D1391358

Books should be returned on or before the
last date stamped below

- 4 DEC 2003

1 7 NOV 2011

2 4 NOV 2004   1 9 AUG 2014

HEADQUARTE 2 4 JAN 2015

1 3 APR 200   17/11/15 HQ

1 6 MAR 2009

ABERDEENSHIRE
LIBRARIES

WITHDRAWN
FROM LIBRARY

F.A.N.Y.

1907

1910

The F.A.N.Y. in Peace and War

The Story of
THE FIRST AID NURSING YEOMANRY
1907–2003

HUGH POPHAM

LEO COOPER

First published in Great Britain 1984 by
LEO COOPER, then an imprint of Secker & Warburg Ltd.

Reissued in this new, revised edition 2003 by
LEO COOPER
an imprint of Pen & Sword Books Ltd,
47 Church Street,
Barnsley,
S. Yorkshire
S70 2AS

Copyright © 2003 by F.A.N.Y. (P.R.V.C.)

ISBN 0 85052 934 4
Line drawings by Tim Jaques

Printed in England by
CPI UK

DEDICATION

This edition is dedicated to the memory of
Sheila Parkinson
Corps Commander 1964–1990

1912

1913

CONTENTS

LIST OF PLATES

Prologue

WHO OR WHAT IS,

OR ARE, OR WERE,

THE FANY?

To answer that convoluted question is one of the purposes of this book. That there is a certain amount of confusion in the matter may be judged from the following remarks recorded during its writing.

'The FANYs? I remember them, of course, during the war. They don't still exist, do they?'

'Weren't they sort of like the ATS?'

'Rather posh girls driving staff cars, I seem to remember.'

'They were started during the Boer War?'

'I had an aunt who was one.'

'Yes, of course I know all about the FANYs. They were widely regarded as sexually sophisticated, but only available to officers of very senior rank.' (This from an ex-RNVR lieutenant.)

'Weren't they the same as the VADs?'

The Japanese were as confused as anyone. This comes from a Tokyo paper of 1946, a time when the FANYs were running a number of canteens for the British and Commonwealth forces occupying the country:

'Four beautiful English ladies wearing khaki uniform over their harmonious bodies talk about their impression of the water paradise, Matsue... FANY, the First Aid Nursing Yeomanry, is an army organized by female patriots of Britain who are proud of an old brilliant tradition and is so famous that it is distinguished among all the British forces... They were as brave and meritorious as "Joan of Arc" in the Crimean War, who is world famous as a brave and gentle nightingale.

'FANY is one of such women's troops and its history is old. It is the

very origin that in 1907 they served in the rear riding on horseback . . .
They usually stayed in British Colonies, but during the Second World
War they showed their active endeavour in the European Front, France
and Belgium and the Far Eastern Front . . . As truck drivers and aeroplane pilots their service did not fall behind men's and some of them are
told, pitifully to say, to have died in the battle.'

Whoever wrote that did not in fact do too badly. He got the title right,
and the date of their founding; and though there is no record of a
FANY Spitfire pilot, they did drive trucks and ambulances in both
world wars, and nurse typhoid cases – like the brave and gentle nightingale – and drag the wounded out of exploding ammunition dumps,
and drop into Occupied Europe as agents, and operate the wireless
sets that maintained contact with them; and some of them, pitifully to
say, did die in the battle.

Moreover, they do still exist, as a small, voluntary well-trained
corps of women with specialized skills of the kind that tend to come
in useful in such emergencies as wars, aircraft crashes, terrorist
bombings, and other 'incidents' of that kind. You will find them, for
instance, training in the Central Casualty and Inquiry Bureau of the
City of London Police, and – if you were allowed in – in certain highly
secret army communications centres. More readily, you might come
across them with their RT sets monitoring the progress of competitors at horse trials, or recording the scores at the TAVR's annual
Courage Trophy, learning first aid and unarmed combat, or in-
terpreting at gatherings of German functionaries and Brazilian trade
delegations and Portuguese military missions.

You won't often see them in uniform, except when training or on
duty with the services, and they don't go in for square-bashing –
though they can march in step when they have to, and they do know
how to salute. They were once described by a senior army officer in
the First World War, in a moment of bafflement, as 'neither fish,
flesh nor fowl but damned good red herring', which may help to
explain the confusion, if not much else. And no, they are not Sloane
Rangers or lesbians or horsey girls from the Shires, or Amazons in
army boots, or rampant feminists. They are modern in the sense that
they have brains and like to use them – and most of them have rather
good jobs – but they are also, some would say quaintly, old-fashioned
in that they feel a sense of responsibility towards the society in which
they live, and if and when this balloon or that goes up, would rather

be doing something constructive than sit about wringing their hands. They also find that learning new skills, or using the ones they have in a different field, in the company of like-minded people, is quite fun. 'And where else, after all,' as one of them remarked, 'can you learn map-reading or orienteering or rifle-shooting or Morse or unarmed combat for a subscription of five pounds a year?'

The FANY's official title – since 1937 – is the Women's Transport Service (FANY). Accurate when it was introduced, it rapidly ceased to be entirely so, and now, when the Corps' main interest is in wireless communications, is almost totally misleading. But as no one has ever used it – except officially – the point is purely academic. The FANYs they have always been, and will remain. If this should strike the reader as odd, one soon learns that almost everything about the FANYs is fairly odd, starting with the fact that their founder was a man, and a man, at that, whose origins and ultimate fate are wrapped in impenetrable mystery, and whose motives, even, are by no means entirely clear. With which opaque but stimulating nugget of information, we may proceed with the story.

ACKNOWLEDGEMENTS

We are delighted that HRH The Princess Royal, Commandant in Chief FANY (PRVC) has provided the Foreword to this revised edition.

The updating of F.A.N.Y. would not have been possible without the help of a number of people who provided new material, read and revised the first edition, researched data and photographs, and gave helpful advice during the preparation of this edition. Particular thanks are extended to Mark Seaman, late of The Imperial War Museum, and to Ailsa Camm, FANY archivist: to Anna Whitehead, Margaret Pawley, and Lynette Beardwood: and to the staff at FANY Headquarters.

I became Commandant-in-Chief in 1981 and in 1984 I was invited to write a foreword to Popham's biography of the Corps, which I did with great pleasure.

My predecessor as Commandant-in-Chief, Princess Alice Countess of Athlone, held the post for much of the Corps' 95 years, including WWII, when the Corps made such a remarkable contribution to victory, gaining no less than 3 awards of the George Cross and 1 George Medal. The efforts of those gallant women have been chronicled in a number of individually dedicated books and films. This new edition covers all aspects of Corps history and describes the remarkable activities that have been undertaken by FANYs from 1907 to 2003. Indeed the change of name in 1999 from WTS (FANY) to FANY (Princess Royal's Volunteer Corps) simply acknowledged the need to reflect wider roles in the Corps title.

To remain relevant and dynamic change is, of course, inevitable and those who read this excellent history should know of the modern day roles that are now being fulfilled by the London based Corps. Support is provided for 2 (National Communication) Signal Brigade in their post-11 September heightened Homeland Security role, and trained personnel continue to be available on a 24 hour call-out basis for both the City of London Police and Army Casualty Bureaux. Apart from these emergency commitments, training opportunities for challenging and adventurous activities are available for FANYs, still volunteers in the true sense.

As we approach the 2007 Centenary, the Corps and its members will be able to celebrate a remarkable past in the knowledge that they are well placed for a varied and often exciting future.

Anne

1913

I

The Sudanese Vision
of the Mysterious Mr Baker
1907

'*To us especially her bravery should appeal. Our mission it is to tend Britain's soldiers on the field, and prove ourselves worthy country-women of the first and greatest of Britain's army nurses.*'

'*It is a great work to ask of a woman . . .*'
Captain E. C. Baker

The oddest fact about the First Aid Nursing Yeomanry Corps is that, at a time when women were fighting hard for political and professional recognition, it should have been founded by a man; and by a man about whom maddeningly little is known. Like a deus ex machina, he appears as, or as having been, a cavalry sergeant-major, with this vision of nurses on horseback forming, as he put it with his endearing predilection for capital letters,

'THE CONNECTING LINK
between the fighting units and the base, where the work of the Field Nurses will go on as it has always done.'

He launches it, achieves some success: then, after half a dozen years, vanishes. Vanishes not merely from the annals of the Corps but apparently from the face of the earth.

For the inspiration behind that connecting link we have only his own brief testimony, as published in the first issue of the official *Gazette* in June 1910:

'During my period of service with Lord Kitchener in the Soudan Campaign, where I had the misfortune to be wounded, it occurred to me that there was a missing link somewhere in the Ambulance Department, which, in spite of the changes in warfare, had not altered very materially since the days of the Crimea when Florence Nightingale and her courageous band of helpers went out

TO SUCCOUR AND SAVE

the wounded.

'On my return from active service I thought out a plan which I anticipated would meet the want, but it was not until September of the year 1907 that I was able to found a troop of young women to see how my ideas on the subject would work . . . but I refused to take the public into my confidence until I was certain that I was progressing

ON THE RIGHT LINES.'

Realist or romantic, patriot or crackpot – or a little of each – Edward Charles Baker and his vision are fairly typical of the period that is known for convenience as the Edwardian Era. Behind the familiar, nostalgic image of elegant, if overdressed, ladies and gentlemen swanning about through a kind of perpetual summer, strange and powerful forces were at work. Too subtle yet too sudden for assimilation, they allowed people, say, to welcome the motor car but not visualize the tank, the aeroplane but not the bombs it would one day drop. Despite wholesale reform of the army and the creation by R. B. Haldane of an Expeditionary Force of 160,000 men capable of being mobilized and fighting within a fortnight, despite the cost in men and money of the South African War, war was still seen as picturesque and stirring, an event that occurred elsewhere, preferably in distant places under wide, hot skies, against tribesmen with spears or ancient flintlock muskets. Thus Baker could, on the one hand, think in terms of women riding sidesaddle round the fringes of a traditional battlefield dressed in vivid scarlet tunics and voluminous skirts; and, on the other, argue prophetically that by doing so they would set free 'all the men who would then be able to take up arms for defence of their homes and country'. But neither he nor anyone else – apart from an obscure Polish banker by the name of I. S. Bloch* – foresaw what the battlefields of 1914–18 would really be like.

But in his impulse to found the Corps, Baker was very much in

---

*As early as 1899 Bloch wrote in a book entitled *Is War Impossible?*: 'Everybody will be entrenched in the next war . . . The spade will be as indispensable to a soldier as his rifle.'

harmony with the times. 'The way seemed open for new impulses of courage and idealism,' wrote R. C. K. Ensor in *England 1870–1914*; and one has merely to note the founding of the Boy Scout Movement in 1907, and the Girl Guides two years later, or of the Voluntary Aid Detachments of the Red Cross which followed Haldane's Territorial and Reserve Forces Act of 1907, or, indeed, of that offshoot of the FANY Corps itself, the Women's Sick and Wounded Convoy Corps, formed by Mrs St Clair Stobart in 1909.

Why it took him nine years to launch his plan Baker nowhere says. A reasonable assumption would be that he remained with his regiment in South Africa for some time after the Sudan campaign, but he was certainly back in England in 1901–2, for his elder son, Ted, was born in 1903.

Ted remembers his father as a giant of a man, six feet seven inches tall, and immensely strong. They lived in London and Ted recalls as a boy learning to ride under his father's eye and being told that he looked like 'a Piccadilly 'ore on a commode': not, one may be sure, a comparison he would have levelled at the ladies of unblemished character whom he recruited into the First Aid Nursing Yeomanry. At some point, also, Baker worked at Smithfield with the Armour Meat Company. 'When I came back from school I always knew when my dad was at home,' Ted says. 'I could get the smell of meat through the letter-box!' But the chronology of these events, and whether Baker was still serving with the colours during the time he was starting the Corps, Ted cannot say.

In a way it is unimportant. Edward Charles Baker fulfilled his destiny by being wounded in the Sudan and, feeling the lack of someone to succour and save him, dreamed up the First Aid Nursing Yeomanry Corps.

ii

'It was solely because of its title Yeomanry I had sought out this corps.'

Grace Ashley-Smith

By advertising in the national newspapers in the autumn of 1907, Baker succeeded in attracting a number of respectable young women to his headquarters in the Gamage's building in Holborn. No details of these early days have survived, but the following salient points appeared in the *Gazette* in November 1910 – by which time, admittedly, the formidable Miss Ashley-Smith from Aberdeen had, as she put it, started fighting for her own way in the office.

Briefly, the Corps' services were to be at the disposal of the Government in the event of hostilities – the irony of this declaration would emerge only when those hostilities began. Members of the Corps had to qualify 'in First Aid and Home Nursing, and in addition go through, and pass, a course of Horsemanship, Veterinary Work, Signalling, and Camp Cookery'. They also had to provide their own uniform and first aid outfit – 'which latter must always be carried when in uniform' – and pay for horse hire. They were to be between seventeen and thirty-five years of age, at least 5ft 3in in height, and had to join for at least one year. There was an enrolment fee of ten shillings, with six shillings a month subscription to the riding school and headquarters, and applicants were required to disclose whether they belonged to any other organization. 'It is not,' Ashley-Smith had stated in a previous issue of the *Gazette*, 'a Corps of shirkers, but of workers... Those who look upon the training of the Corps as a pleasant pastime are advised to think twice before offering themselves at headquarters as recruits.'

No such strictures, one suspects, were laid down initially. At all events, by May 1908 the Corps was sufficiently in being to be inspected by a certain Colonel F. C. Ricardo at the riding school. Having been previously unaware of its existence, he duly expressed his surprise and approval, and invited the Corps members to attend the Royal Naval and Military Tournament which was then in progress. 'The troop's appearance there,' Baker wrote later, 'aroused the interest of the public, and applications from prospective recruits came pouring in from all parts of the country.'

In February 1909, Baker's eldest daughter entered the fray. Sergeant-Major Katie Baker – to give her her full, honorary title – personally tackled the problem of recruitment and, according to her father, 'increased the great public interest by recruiting for the Corps at Whitehall, where she stood with the Recruiting Sergeants of His Majesty's Regular Forces'. The results were so 'gratifying', Baker wrote a year later, that

'the Corps has reached the highest possible stage of efficiency, and is
READY TO TAKE THE FIELD
at a moment's notice.'

This was, to put it mildly, pure hyperbole, for by 1910 the Corps had fallen apart, as we shall see in due course.

It is, however, undoubtedly true that the year 1909 marked the first flowering of the First Aid Nursing Yeomanry Corps. A constitution was drawn up, under which 'Captain Baker' as he now described himself would be promoted to (honorary) Major when membership reached 250 and (honorary) Colonel when it reached 500; membership then was about 100. The smart headed notepaper now gave the Corps' address as 118–122 Holborn, rather than the Gamage's building; and under the crest, with 'Captain E. C. Baker, CO' were listed a Captain L. C. V. Hardwicke, MD, RAMCT, as adviser on First Aid and Ambulance; a medical officer; a vet, and no less than four riding schools.

In June 1909 a charity matinée in aid of the Corps was held at the St James's Theatre, London. Of the sixty patrons named on the programme – among them Mrs W. H. Asquith – twenty had titles and twenty-five had military or naval rank, including that same Grenadier Colonel, F. C. Ricardo. Two of the one-act plays presented were by Mrs St Clair Stobart (whom we shall soon meet again in less jolly circumstances); Harry Tate gave 'his famous sketch, "Motoring"'; and *Mr* Harry Lauder sang 'She's My Daisy' and 'The Wedding o' Sandy McNab'. The show raised £170, which was to be devoted to the purchase of an ambulance wagon and to help provide headquarters. But this sum was never paid into the Corps' bank.

The details of the row that blew up after the charity matinée are somewhat conjectural, but the gist of the matter is clear. Some members of the Corps were becoming increasingly dissatisfied with the leadership of their commanding officer. In July 1909 Baker wrote a slightly pained open letter to the membership, complaining that a cabal had been formed, the intention of which was to put the management into the hands of an executive committee on which neither Baker nor his daughter would be represented.

Money, almost certainly, was at the root of it. In the same letter, Baker mentions an earlier meeting 'in reference to the Matinée money, as the Corps was short of funds, and the Ambulance Wagon was not paid for'. The reference to the ambulance would be unremarkable but for a letter of April 5th, 1909, from a Kathleen Maclean Darcy to Captain Baker which states quite firmly: 'I will be pleased to provide you with your wagon. I understand the cost will be £100 which amount I will send you later.' What had become of the £170? Indeed, what had become of Kathleen Maclean Darcy and her £100?

Well, we do know what happened eventually to the first sum, for on December 15th, 1909, a document of indemnity was accepted by 'Mrs St Clair Stobart and that section of the First Aid Nursing Yeomanry Corps who have disassociated themselves from the Section of the Corps of which Captain Baker is in Command'. 'That section', led by Mrs Stobart, had become the Women's Sick and Wounded Convoy Corps, and Mrs Stobart had deposited the £170 'in the names of the Trustees' – unidentified. Now, on payment of £85 to Baker, the new formation was relieved of any liabilities it might have incurred for ambulances etc: relieved, too, of any right to use the name or crest of the First Aid Nursing Yeomanry Corps. The indemnity was signed by Ethel Temperley, Flora Sanders, Lucy W. Hawkins and M. A. Stobart, 'Members of the Executive Committee of the Women's Sick and Wounded Convoy Corps', who had broken away from the original Corps and taken a great many of its members with them.*

The conclusion must be that poor Captain Baker had collected, on the one hand, a bunch of well-to-do, horsey girls who had been attracted to his Corps by the lure of the riding, the glamour of the uniform, and his romantic notions; and, on the other, a group of much tougher and more practical young women whose ideas were equally patriotic

*Mrs Stobart took her Convoy Corps to the Balkan War of 1912. Two years later she started another unit, the Women's National Service League, which was rejected by the Red Cross and so, like the FANY, was forced to operate independently, first in France and Belgium, and later back in the Balkans. (See *Women in Uniform*, Elizabeth Ewing.)

but rather less picturesque. When the latter left – significantly to don the Convoy Corps' extremely sensible uniform of 'divided skirt, Norfolk golf jacket and helmet' – most of the others simply drifted away. Such was the sorry condition of the First Aid Nursing Yeomanry Corps at the beginning of 1910 when that one word 'Yeomanry' caught the interest of an able and energetic young Scots woman, Grace Ashley-Smith.

1914

2

O Dreams! O Destinations!
1910–1914
I · THE DREAMS

'When I joined there were three present at my first stretcher drill, and six at my first riding drill . . . One good lady offered to give me hints on riding. We solemnly mounted, and rode round and round at a slow walk, and then at a gentle trot . . . We quickened the trot, and for some reason I could not solve, the lady who had offered me tips fell off. She did so twice. I was congratulated on riding an unmanageable horse. I left that parade in a thoughtful mood.'
Grace Ashley-Smith

The renascence, indeed almost the second founding, of the Corps may be traced to the recruitment of Ashley-Smith.* Baker remained the titular commanding officer for a further two years; but increasingly from 1911 onwards Lilian Franklin, who had joined in 1909, and Grace Ashley-Smith established their dominance. 'Was it a Scottish reluctance to losing my guineas, was it merely Destiny that made me remain?' the latter mused in her recollections of those early days, and left the question unanswered. Once joined, she soon started 'to fight for her own way in the office'.

The elegant, but not very practical, uniform was replaced by a divided khaki skirt (with 'patent fasteners') worn over riding breeches and a khaki tunic, and riding sidesaddle was abandoned in favour of astride. Training, based on RAMC practice, was adopted,

---

*It was normal practice in the Corps for members to refer to each other by surname only. First names were rarely used – so rarely that they are often difficult to establish.

and there was no more talk of 'riding on battlefields'. Ashley-Smith founded, and for five issues sustained at her own expense, a trim little magazine entitled *Women and War: Official Gazette of the First Aid Nursing Yeomanry Corps and Cadet Yeomanry* (the latter was a separate organization, also founded by Baker, for boys from twelve to seventeen); but even at £6 10s 0d for 250 copies she found it too expensive, and it folded in November 1910.

The highlight of the training year was the annual camp. In September 1910 Baker wrote to the *Daily Mail*, correcting a report that the ubiquitous Mrs Stobart's Women's Sick and Wounded Convoy Corps camp at Swanage was 'the first time in history probably' that a company of women would 'go under canvas, military fashion'. Not so, said Captain Baker: 'That Corps is an offshoot of the First Aid Nursing Yeomanry Corps, founded by myself over two years ago, and we have already had two camps, at one of which . . . Mrs Stobart acted as quartermaster.'

The first camp apparently took place in the grounds of a private estate in Chiddingfold in Surrey, and there is a photograph of fourteen uniformed girls posing glumly in front of a tent. In the *Gazette* for June 1910 it was announced that the Corps would be going to camp – place unspecified – at the end of July for eight days; but no report survives. Diversions included 'wounded rescue races' in which the 'wounded' reclined in postures of realistic agony, and the 'rescuers' galloped up, treated them appropriately, and, if the 'wounds' permitted, pushed and shoved them into the saddle and led them in; and night route-marches with stretchers which turned into a sort of treasure-hunt for casualties. Each one bore a label describing her wound, and on return the rescuer had to describe the condition and the treatment required. One victim, rather overdoing her sufferings, was tersely described as 'drunk and disorderly'. Everyone enjoyed themselves; they worked hard – reveille was often at 5.30am – and took the training seriously. For relaxation and refreshment there was a Canteen with Devonshire Cider (3½d per bottle), Beer (3d a bottle), Fry's chocolate, mixed fruit drops, and Sugar for the Horses, 1d per packet.

A strong impression emerges from these years before the war of a band of resourceful and enthusiastic young women searching desperately for recognition and a role. The problem was to sustain that enthusiasm in the face of scepticism from officialdom – not to mention the jeers of the populace, to whom the sight of a woman in uniform was a subject for incredulous ribaldry. Therefore they tried everything in order to establish a presence. Early on they attended the Derby hoping against hope that someone would faint or be mauled by a horse; without results. They took part in a pony gymkhana at Ranelagh and put on 'an excellent display', and a 'Military Tournament and Torchlight Tattoo at Brighton', where twenty-six Corps members gave an ambulance display and several competed in the jumping. They rode, accompanied by the ambulance wagon, from London to St Albans and back. One rather more ambitious scheme deserves a mention, even though it never materialized: this was to ride in convoy from London to Edinburgh.

The idea was first mooted in August 1910, the intention being to prove that the Corps was not composed of 'fair-weather soldiers', but that 'in the event of an invasion – say on the Scotch coast' and probable breakdown of the railway system, they would still be able to arrive where they were needed. The CO, by now apparently sure that he was on the right lines, sent a letter describing the plan – under the heading 'Are there any Florence Nightingales left?' – to no less than eleven national newspapers, most of which printed it. But he quickly ran into trouble within the Corps, notably from his newly promoted sergeant, Grace Ashley-Smith. While enthusiastic in principle, she saw the practical difficulties, as well as the unwisdom of announcing their intentions in advance.

'This route march to Scotland,' she wrote to Katie Baker, 'seems to me impossible . . .' and went on to enumerate the objections: the distance; the lateness of the season (November); the difficulty of finding suitable horses; and, not least, the expense. She followed this up with a letter to Baker himself, which seems to have had its intended effect, for no more is heard of the proposal.

The funeral of Edward VII in May 1910 seemed to present another opportunity for establishing the Corps' identity. Two of the girls went to Buckingham Palace in full uniform to present a wreath, a gesture that was later acknowledged personally by Queen Alexandra; and Baker offered the ambulance 'fully equipped with stretchers and bearer party, and Trained Nurses' to the Metropolitan Police, to stand by at the funeral itself. The offer was refused. A number of the girls were out independently, however, during the Lying-in-State, and rendered 'First Aid to the fainting'.

Nothing seemed to go quite right that year. Active members could be numbered on the fingers of two hands, and Baker's vision of a Corps ready to take the field at a moment's notice was no more than a mirage glimmering above the desert sands.

ii

'In 1911 things progressed slowly, and it was not until
1912 the Corps began to make real progress . . .'
Grace Ashley-Smith

Of the power struggle that undoubtedly went on within the Corps during those two years, the only conclusive evidence is its outcome. But there are, here and there, hints and clues as to what was transpiring at 118–122 Holborn, particularly during 1911.

In February 1911 a letter in which the Duke of Argyll declines to become 'President or Patron' of the Corps is addressed to 'Miss Franklin'; and one in March in which Lord Valentia 'is delighted to become a Patron of yr very excellent movement' is addressed to 'Madam'. Previously such letters would have been addressed to Captain Baker or to Katie. The Corps, it would seem, was now being run by Franklin and Ashley-Smith.

What is certain is that in 1911 the latter rented a flat at 83 Lexham Gardens, South Kensington, 'which we used as a Headquarters Office, and where we met for signalling and stretcher drill until we increased our number so much we had to hold drills in the Surrey Yeomanry Riding School'.

The final break with the Bakers took place – not without some hard feelings on the part of the founder and his daughter – on January 6th, 1912, when according to Ashley-Smith's Regimental Order Book there was an 'Inspection of Corps by Colonel Ricardo at which he formally took over command of the Corps'. Present on this momentous occasion were: Franklin (Second Lieutenant), Smith (Sergeant-Major), Walton (Sergeant), Wicks (Corporal), Anderson, Bennett, Birch and Ball. The First Aid Nursing Yeomanry was under new management.

'I arranged for RAMC Sergeants to give us stretcher drill and teach us bandaging and a signalling officer to give us semaphore and Morse. Then I applied to Houndslow [sic] Barracks and got permission for the Corps to ride there, and get cavalry drill from the Sergeant-Major of the 19th Hussars, in addition to the recruits at the Surrey Yeomanry Headquarters for riding.' Grace Ashley-Smith was, there is no doubt about it, a genius at arranging things. Pat Waddell describes her as 'a tall pleasant woman with a Scottish accent': from her photograph in uniform – used in an advertisement in the *Gazette* for Sandow's corsets – she appears as a handsome young woman, with a mass of curly brown hair, wide-set eyes, and a firm mouth with a hint of humour at the corners: the face of a woman accustomed to getting her own way.

'The Corps continued to train, often under great difficulties,' she wrote of these immediate pre-war years. 'Numbers rose and dwindled, but some did not give in.' The camps continued, both at weekends and in the summer: at Haslemere and Bourne End in 1912, at Pirbright in 1913 and '14; and from Ashley-Smith's stern, scribbled orders ('Officers' Orderlies' – she and Franklin were now lieutenants – 'will make the beds in the officers' tents, clean their boots each morning, & polish the brass on their belts'; 'Cole Hamilton and Cluff to have ready in Dixon's cart 9 horse nosebags with feeds...') certain names recur: Margaret Cole-Hamilton and Nora Cluff; Cecily Mordaunt; Isabel Wicks; Edith Walton; Pat Waddell; Grace Anderson; Mary Lewis.

At Pirbright the Brigade of Guards took the Corps 'under their wing', as Ashley-Smith put it; lent them tents and all the other gear they needed – no more hiring from the Army & Navy Stores, though they still had to hire a field (for fifteen shillings) and employ a 'Sanitary man' (four shillings) – and laid on suitably hefty troopers to act as casualties. 'Everyone loved the camps,' Ashley-Smith wrote, 'we had a heavenly time, lots of hard work and discomfort, but unfailing cheerfulness and fun and good fellowship.' Though they were a voluntary organization, with no official standing, they could reasonably feel that they had at last attained recognition, an identity, a role: all the more so when, at their last camp before the war, they not only took part in manoeuvres, but attended the Guards' Church Parade – an unprecedented honour. 'It was worth all the labour and slogging, and self-denial and discouragement – all the ups and downs, all the jeers and sneers and laughter – to be there at last – part of the army –

yes and with the best of it.' After that, official rejection, when it came, would be all the more galling.

The first chance for active service came with the introduction of the third Home Rule Bill for Ireland in 1912, and the adamant opposition to it, orchestrated by Sir Edward Carson, of the Ulster Unionists. Civil war seemed imminent; and in June 1913, Ashley-Smith wrote to Carson, offering the Corps' services 'to help with the wounded', and adding with a rather charming naïveté: 'If this offer should not have been made to you will you kindly forward it to the proper quarter.'

Nothing came of it, of course, for that little war was to suffer postponement in deference to another, on a rather grander scale; but the Corps received considerable publicity as a result of their offer. In the *London Budget* for November 2nd, 1913, for example, Ashley-Smith's picture appears with those of Lady Kilmorey, Lady Castlereagh, the Dowager Lady Smiley and the Marchioness of Londonderry – two of whom had recently consented to become patronesses of the Corps. There is a photograph of three FANYs loading a stretcher into a horse-drawn ambulance; and Ashley-Smith, described for the first time as 'Organizing Officer' of the Corps, explains that it consists of 'thirty-five gentlewomen, and is really a women's mounted ambulance corps'.

An even more compelling suggestion of having, at last, 'made it', came at the end of the 1914 summer camp. Through the good offices of Major Smallman of the RAMC, Surgeon-General Woodhouse was induced to come and inspect them. Rather grumpily, being under the impression that they were VADs, he said he would give them half an hour. However, with the collusion of their RAMC instructor, Sergeant Pepper, the girls put on such an impressive show of medical expertise that he stayed to tea, and ended up by recommending Ashley-Smith to go and see Sir Arthur Sloggett, Chief Commissioner of the Red Cross, at the War Office. She duly went, was cordially received, and described to him the Corps and its purpose. From that interview she went away with the reasonable conviction that if and when war came, the First Aid Nursing Yeomanry would receive a sympathetic hearing at the highest level of the army's medical services. In the meantime, happy in this assumption, and leaving the Corps' affairs in the experienced hands of Lilian Franklin, she sailed for South Africa to visit her sister.

Was the Corps that she now left behind her ready, as Captain Baker would have had one believe four years before, to take the field at a moment's notice? And what field? The score or so members who attended the camps had undoubtedly trained hard and were skilled in their particular disciplines: more important, they were the kind of people who were willing to take on whatever job turned up. Which was fortunate since they could no more visualize, in July 1914, what those jobs would be, than Baker could in 1907. What they also possessed, in addition to training and enthusiasm, was loyalty to the FANY. But, precious as this quality is to any unit, it does tend to limit objectivity. Compare it, for instance, with the Voluntary Aid Detachments (VADs). Formed two years after the FANY, by 1914 they consisted of 2500 branches with 74,000 voluntary members, and they had direct links with the Territorial Force as well as being a limb of the British Red Cross Society. In contrast, the FANY had only 30 or 40 members, and no official sponsors of any kind: in fact, probably the only reason that many of them had joined the FANY Corps and not the VADs was that magic word 'Yeomanry'. It is a tribute to the staunchness and persistence of that little band of pioneers that the FANY not only survived as an independent formation in the face of indifference and hostility, but was soon being acclaimed for its work.

3

O Dreams! O Destinations!
1914–15
II · THE DESTINATIONS

'*Now God be thanked who has matched us with this hour.*'

Rupert Brooke

When war was declared on August 4th, 1914, Grace Ashley-Smith was aboard the *Edinburgh Castle* on her way to South Africa. She promptly sent a wireless message to Cape Town to book her passage home. She was actually ashore for about four hours, thus setting from the outset the cracking pace she was to keep up throughout the war.

Meanwhile Lilian Franklin and Edith Walton in London quickly followed up their Army contacts; but Sir Arthur Sloggett, who had been friendly enough before, had nothing to suggest for the Corps. If they had known of the reception that other women were getting from the Services at that time, they might have been even angrier than they were. Vera Laughton Mathews, applying to the Admiralty for any job, however humble, was curtly told: 'We don't want any petticoats here.' (She had her revenge later by becoming Director of the WRNS.) And Dr Elsie Inglis, when she offered to take a qualified medical team to the front, received the even more chilling reply: 'My good lady, go home and sit still!'★

★One should be cautious of feeling too smug about these reactions. Judith Chisholm, the pilot who in 1980 set the record for a woman's solo flight to Australia, recounted in *The Times* (January 19th, 1983) how, with 2000 hours on type, she offered her services in an emergency to Shell, to be told that their passengers 'would not like it if a little blonde dollybird started to fly the aeroplane'.

So the members of the Corps – still numbering fewer than thirty – had to content themselves for the time being with more ladylike occupations such as sewing parties. More to their taste, they also gathered equipment together in anticipation of an official change of heart. This was how Ashley-Smith found them when she returned to London in early September.

But Ashley-Smith was not prepared to wait. As luck would have it, one of her shipmates on the voyage home was the Belgian Minister for the Colonies, Louis Franck. He had regaled her with the latest information from Belgium, and thus sown the seeds of future action. In London she learnt that there was a British field hospital already at work in Antwerp, and she immediately rushed off to see the secretary and offered the Corps. He was no more encouraging than the War Office, but grudgingly agreed that she could go if she could get a passport – which he was fairly sure she could not. Two days later, in uniform, she was in Antwerp and reporting for duty.

In this characteristically unorthodox manner the FANYs secured their first toehold where the action was; and very soon the Belgians were offering Ashley-Smith a 300-bed hospital, if only she could bring the rest of the Corps over. She promptly telegraphed Lilian Franklin to that effect; but it was already too late.

ii

'I wish my mother could see me now,
With a grease gun under my car,
Filling the differential
Ere I start for the sea afar,
A-top a sheet of frozen iron, in cold that would make
*   you cry.*
I used to be in Society once
Danced and hunted and flirted once,
Had white hands and complexion once,
Now I am FANY.'

(*Gazette*)

By the end of September the Germans were at the gates of Antwerp, and the bombardment, which was to last for twelve days, had begun. Ashley-Smith was at once caught up in the confusion of retreat, working in the hospital and picking up wounded from the surrounding battlefields, often under fire. The defence of the city by the Belgian army – and 3000 Marines sent in by Churchill – held up the German advance but could not halt it. The city fell on October 10th, Ghent a few days later; and Ashley-Smith, who had gone back to succour, and subsequently bury, a wounded British officer, found herself sharing a billet with a number of very surprised German soldiers. A woman in uniform was as great a novelty to them as it was to the British: a British woman in uniform there, at that moment, was *verblüffend*. The local German commander refused her a laissez-passer, but also failed to lock her up, so she contacted a Belgian baroness whom she happened to know, and she engineered her escape through Holland. By the middle of October she was back in London and eager to get the first contingent of FANYs to the Continent as soon as possible.

She managed to acquire a brand-new motor ambulance* inside a week – something even the War Office couldn't do – and cajoled Sir Arthur Stanley, a Council Member of the British Red Cross, into arranging permits for the FANYs, the ambulance and herself to cross to Calais on the Red Cross yacht.

The party that set off for Folkestone on October 26th, 1914, numbered exactly twelve: six FANYs – one of them the invaluable Sister Wicks – three nurses, two men dressers, and Ashley-Smith's brother Bill driving the ambulance. A delay at the docks gave them their first taste of genuine casualties. In the face of an insufferable colonel who questioned the usefulness of 'their soft white hands', they helped to carry stretcher-cases from a temporary hospital in the Pavilion Hotel to the ambulances. Then, as the Red Cross yacht was not running, they finally crossed to Calais on the regular ferry on October 27th. The wartime service of the First Aid Nursing Yeomanry Corps had begun.

*This was sharp of her, for at that time there were very few motor ambulances in France, so she had virtually guaranteed their welcome.

iii

'Dear dirty old Lamarck!'

Calais was a seething mass of trains, horses, gun-limbers, carts, refugees, and soldiers either on their way to the front or, wounded, on their way back from it. Less than fifty miles to the west the first battle of Ypres, which had started ten days before with a powerful and determined German offensive, was about to reach crisis point with the Allied commanders, Foch, French, Haig, Rawlinson, desperately struggling to plug the gaps in the line. Casualties had been heavy: 8000 were evacuated through Calais alone during the first five days that the FANYs were there. 'Calais swept by storms of wind and rain, cold and wet and cheerless,' as Ashley-Smith wrote later; 'the Calais along whose quais one never-to-be-forgotten night, rows of wounded lay, in the darkness and the cold and the rain.'

In this chaos the FANYs were allocated to a shabby convent school opposite the Cathedral and known as Lamarck, which had been taken over by the Belgians and was being run by a scratch staff of British and Belgian doctors, Sisters of Mercy and Belgian orderlies. 'Hospital' was a courtesy title: the beds were straw-filled palliasses laid out on the floor, and the patients – a hundred of them, many suffering from typhoid – were ranged cheek by jowl in the two three-storey buildings. The FANYs were immediately enrolled as probationers, and their ambulance was in constant use.

It was a daunting and squalid induction for those 'gently-bred high-spirited girls', but now there was no time to think, no time for regrets; there was too much to do. 'Week by week, day and night, they went about their monotonous task – for typhoid is not a romantic service – and to it they gave their hearts, high courage and patience and unselfish devotion.' That, allowing for Ashley-Smith's tendency towards purple prose, is not a bad tribute.

Lamarck occupies a unique place in the annals of the Corps. They were there in increasing numbers for a full two years; and the experience engendered a tradition of versatility, of doing whatever job came to hand, no matter how unfamiliar, tough or revolting, that has persisted to the present day. It also created a special bond between the Corps and the Belgians: if it had not been for them, the FANYs always felt, the Corps might not have survived as an independent body, nor found its own particular niche in the war effort.

Pat Waddell, who arrived there in February 1915, described her first impressions of it: 'A row of latrines faced the main entrance to the convent school just inside the gateway... There was a stone-flagged kitchen on the right with a sanded floor which appeared to be the dining-room; opposite it was a door marked *Salle I* printed on it, and a stone staircase led to the floors above...' One can almost smell it, that peculiarly French pot-pourri of bad drains and garlic, with just a whiff of disinfectant from the wards above.

To begin with the FANYs had trouble finding billets. 'The French civilians,' Ashley-Smith wrote, 'hated the English people and resented our presence; they hated the Belgians and were furious with the English for coming to nurse them.' When they did find some grumpy madame prepared to let them a room it was never for more than two or three days – fear of spies was the reason given – after which they had to go through the same disheartening business all over again. However, they at last succeeded in renting an empty shop with the auspicious name of Le Bon Génie. 'When our people at home first heard that we were "sleeping in a shop window",' Pat Waddell wrote, 'they were mildly startled, but the window-panes were completely pasted over with brown paper. We were so short of beds that the night-nurses tumbled into the day-nurses' beds as soon as they were vacated in the morning...' And there was, of course, no bath. There was no running water in the hospital, come to that; it all had to be drawn from a pump in the yard.

So rife was typhoid among the patients that three wards on the ground floor were turned over exclusively to them, the only such wards in Calais at that time. These gaunt, delirious creatures who raved and cried – and occasionally tried to strangle their benefactors – were enough to try the nerves of seasoned nurses, but the girls coped; indeed 'coping' almost became a Corps motto in time. 'Untrained, yes, but teachable,' the redoubtable Sister Wicks wrote of them. 'When I think of the spongings these children have to do, with the basin on the floor as there are no chairs – back-aching work; then the two-hourly feeds which can only be given sip by sip, the injections and routine work, I wonder how they do it.' They probably wondered themselves.

Variety, in an unwelcome form, came first from the air, in the leisurely, menacing shape of the Zeppelins. The first raid, in February

1915, did little damage; the second, a month later, dropped a bomb on the Cathedral, destroying the Lady Chapel and blowing out every window in the hospital. As it was snowing at the time, and most of the beds were littered with broken glass, and the male orderlies had prudently taken to the cellars, the girls had their work cut out. Altogether Calais was subjected to more than ninety air raids and two bombardments from the sea during the course of the war; but this was the nearest Lamarck came to being hit, and none of the girls was seriously hurt in any of the raids.

Variety in another guise came from routine trips to the front to dish out comforts to the troops – shirts, mufflers and socks. Especially socks. The provenance of these particular comforts is revealed in an intriguing note in the *Gazette*: 'The large supply of knitted body-belts sent to headquarters early in the war have gradually been made into socks by Mr Rowsell.' It was not unusual for the girls to come under shellfire on these occasions, nor for the ambulance that they had driven up from base full of Mr Rowsell's recycled body-belts to go back with a freight of injured men.

Even without the shellfire these trips were fairly arduous. The vehicles were of the kind now only seen on the London to Brighton run, with rudimentary windscreens or none, brutal springing, uncertain engines, no self-starters, and tyres depressingly prone to punctures. In these bone-shakers, on tiny oil sidelights (the carbide headlights, and sometimes even the sidelights, were forbidden), they drove on narrow roads with deep mud on either side, constantly having to dodge other traffic, staff cars, gun-limbers, horses, and tramping men. Luckily when they did slide off the hard surface, there was usually a cheerful mob of soldiers to heave them out of the morass. The landscape, all gutted houses and stricken trees, was rendered even more desolate by the inundations engineered by the Belgians back in September to halt the German advance.

At this time the FANYs were the only women driving in France: the effect of this on the soldiers is adequately summed up by one wounded man who, on recovering consciousness after a gas attack, opened his eyes and exclaimed in awed tones: 'My Gawd, it's a woman!'

For two of the girls, Beryl Hutchinson and Mary Lewis, one of these trips to the front was more harassing than most.

They were summoned at short notice to take the *auto-cuisine* – or motorized soup-kitchen – to nourish the 7th Regiment of Belgian Mounted Artillery, attached to the British 5th Division, which was about to start for the front. What this meant was that for a week or more they trundled along in the wake of the guns and horses at a speed of 20km a day; and when they bivouacked for the night, were expected to cook something edible for 140 men on what amounted to one temperamental Primus stove.

On they trailed, out of France and into Flanders, into Ypres and out again to Hellfire Corner, where, on May 24th, 1915, they came under attack by gas.* 'Out of a green haze that hung over everything one unending stream of Tommies, English and Scotch, came down the road, tottering, stumbling, gasping.' Fortunately the two girls had (Belgian) respirators, while many of the men had none, and they spent the next six hours doing what they could to relieve the collapsed and retching men.

iv

' "F-A-N-Y" spelt a passing Tommy as he leant from the train. "Fanny!† Huh, I wonder what that stands for?" "First anywhere," suggested another.'

From *Fanny Went to War*

Work in the Rue de la Rivière continued unabated throughout 1915. They now had a fairly motley fleet of vehicles with which to provide both routine and anything but routine services: in addition to the *auto-cuisine* there were now three ambulances – converted motor-cars – with a fourth on the way, a lorry, and, the most splendid contraption of all, a Brown, Hughes & Strachan Motor-Bath. This remarkable vehicle, supplied by Marian and Hope Gamwell – of whom more later – consisted of a 40hp Daimler to the chassis of which had been fitted a boiler fired by 'two special furnaces', twelve collapsible canvas baths, six a side, a tank, a pump, and a canvas screen to preserve the bathers' modesty. Even more incredibly, it actually worked, both as a motor and as an ablution. Two girls,

*This is often referred to as 'the first gas attack', but that took place a month earlier, on April 22nd. Gas was, in fact, used sporadically throughout Second Ypres – a forlorn battle that cost the British 60,000 casualties and achieved nothing.
†'Fanny' had at this time none of its later, impolite connotations, either British or American.

having started it by hand, manoeuvred this monster all round the Calais area, on one occasion 'bathing' 600 men in two days. The report of that ablutionary marathon ends: 'James [as the juggernaut was fondly christened] had sunk in the mud and had to be towed out with horses. After breaking three sets of chains and sideslipping into the farm midden, we once more reached the road and set off for Calais *and a wash.*'

This, like so many incidents of the time, tells much about the girls themselves. Perhaps because they were all volunteers and unpaid, they give the sense of tremendous *joie de vivre*, even in circumstances where *joie* of any kind might be thought to be in short supply. No one should be deluded by this insouciance, however; although the work was hard and often unpleasant, they devoted themselves to it, heart and soul. As one of them wrote in the *Gazette* in July 1915: 'All the old arguments against women serving at the front have been proved invalid.'

'Soft white hands' indeed!

1914–18

4

Convalescents, Convoys and Canteens
1915–1916

'*As disillusion came and the war dragged on with its toil of death and devastation, manpower shortages became increasingly acute and women whose endeavours to help in the war effort had been spurned were sought out by the government and other authorities with a zeal exceeding their own . . . But it was caused not by enlightened attitudes but the dire needs of the moment.*'
Elizabeth Ewing: Women in Uniform

In January 1915 Grace Ashley-Smith found time to get married: thereafter she was Mrs MacDougall or, to her friends, simply Mac. As far as the FANYs were concerned, however, marriage diminished her energy and enthusiasm not one jot. While the staff at Lamarck continued to nurse the *blessés* (wounded) and *typhiques* (typhoid cases), she raced round trying to drum up more work for the Corps. In this she was sometimes embarrassingly successful.

The first result of her peregrinations may be traced to May of 1915, in a letter written in her fluent but somewhat flatfooted French to General Clooten, Belgian CO of Calais Base:

'En suite de mon voyage au Camp du Ruchard je viens vous demander le permission d'installer une "messe" pour les sept cents convalescents typhiques la-bas.'

These wretches, she told the General, were half-starved, and she proposed to supplement their miserable diet with '*bouillon, café au lait avec du pain and des biscuits*' at set hours. In addition she would supply '*cigs, choc et d'autres petites choses*', and such comforts as canvas chairs, a gramophone, writing paper, magazines and books. In the event, the FANYs did even better, as will appear.

This handsome offer was eventually, in the General's own words, 'sealed with a closely definite situation'; and the canteen duly opened for business, with Margaret Cole-Hamilton in command, three FANYs and one trained nurse, about the end of August, and with an inaugural concert. The scheme was an instant success, which is hardly surprising since Ruchard, stuck out in the 'Salisbury Plain of France', was miles from the nearest town, and there was nothing for the inmates to do except go quietly mad. Arrests for a variety of offences which had been running at twenty a day went down to two. Nor were their prices excessive, with tea, coffee and cocoa at 5 centimes a mug.

For the girls themselves this hutted camp in the middle of nowhere lacked even the questionable attractions of wartime Calais. Janette Lean, the Corps secretary, who paid the camp a visit in the spring of 1916, was shocked at the chill, damp quarters they had to live in. 'The fact of the girls roughing it so much,' she wrote, 'had only done us harm in the eyes of the Belgians, as they thought that was how we live at home.'

The original five were joined quite soon by the formidable and ubiquitous Lady Constance Baird. On first offering her services to the FANYs she had proposed being accompanied by her maid; but when this was discouraged, travelled with a hip-flask instead and with this was used to lift the spirits of her patients, libations which ensured her popularity. Despite these quirks, she proved a valuable addition to the strength, helping Nurse Lovell on the TB wards.

Even more to the point than Lady Baird's hip-flask was the cinema. Adèle Crockett, who took over from Margaret Cole-Hamilton, described this machine and its attendant problems. It had cost the FANYs 2000fr to buy, and a further 145fr a week to run. The projector had its own generator, which was very heavy on *essence* but at least it supplied the canteen with electric light as well; '. . . and for it you must have a competent motor mechanic to work the motor and a proper cinema operator, also another to help a bit, otherwise there is a risk of the films catching fire and getting destroyed, also setting fire to the building.'

And, suddenly, one has a vivid little picture of this dreary, wind-swept camp, the crowd of Belgian *poilus* in every stage of convalescence struggling through the rain and mud to the canteen to watch the flickering picture-show under the supervision of an anxious Australian girl who must quite often have marvelled at the fate that had landed her there – in between worrying whether the whole place was going to go up in flames.

After a long and distracting period of rumours, Ruchard was at last taken over by the French in June 1917, and the FANYs moved to the Hôpital Militaire Belge at Soligny-la-Trappe in the Department of Orne, ninety miles west of Paris. But Soligny was never a success – there were never the numbers of battle casualties there to justify, as Crockett put it, 'the inconveniences and the absolute want of outside distraction' – and closed after six months.

ii

'Crank! Crank! You Fanys!
Stand to your buses again –
Snatch up the stretchers and blankets,
Down to the barge through the rain!
Up go the planes in the dawning!
Up go the cars to stand by –
There's many a job for the wounded,
    Forward the F.A.N.Y.!'

The First Aid Nursing Yeomanry Corps had always visualized itself as working with and for the British Army. That was its *raison d'être*, implicit in its conception, and confirmed by its close links with the Guards Regiments, especially the Blues. But what had seemed obvious to the girls in those jolly days before 1914, evaporated in the sudden, fierce heat of war. There were two reasons for the blank wall of official obstruction that faced the FANYs when they first tried to put their training to good use. The first was the inability of the military mind to picture women in any wartime role except nursing – and it was only Florence Nightingale at Scutari who had compelled it to rec-ognize them in that capacity. The second reason lay in the fiercely independent nature of the Corps itself. In a note written in August 1915, the Director General of the Army Medical Service, Sir Alfred Keogh, commented to Sir Arthur Sloggett, then Chief Commissioner of the British Red Cross Society, and always amiable towards the Corps: 'It is rather difficult to find a place for these young women as they will not place themselves under the auspices of the BRCS. If they would only do this I feel certain we could find employment for them in one or other of our bases. The IGC will not have anything to do with these irregular units.' Forwarding the note to Mac, Sloggett scribbled on the back: 'Dear Mrs MacDougall, you see what the IGC says – wouldn't you *like* to join the Red Cross?'

This had followed yet another attempt by Mac to persuade the War Office to use FANY drivers in place of men on the ambulances in France, and its routine refusal. But, as Mac herself remarked in a notable mixed metaphor, 'Red tape never cut any ice with me.' Her answer to Sloggett's question would have been a cautious 'Possibly' – if that was the only way to achieve their primary ambition, so be it – and during the latter half of 1915 an agreement was worked out between the FANY and the Joint War Committee of the British Red Cross Society and the Order of St John of Jerusalem, the latter two organizations having teamed up for the duration.

In essence, the Corps was now to be employed or 'commissioned' by the BRCS 'to provide transport for the British sick and wounded at Calais'. The BRCS would provide the vehicles, tools, stores and so forth, and, subject to BRCS approval, the Corps would provide the drivers. They would wear their own uniform and would receive the same 'privileges and concessions' as other members of the BRCS. This agreement, with certain modifications and amendments, enabled the FANY, under the command of Lilian Franklin, to run the Calais Convoy for the British from January 1st, 1916, until the Armistice.

The compromise was reasonable. The function of the British Red Cross Society at that time was firstly to supplement what could be supplied by the RAMC, and secondly 'to co-ordinate and bring together under a single administration all voluntary efforts for the relief and comfort of the sick and wounded in war'.

And that, in the view of the Executive Committee of the BRCS, should include the FANYs.

'The site of the convoy was on a hill outside the town, halfway to the

Casino which was on the front . . . In peace time it must have been a pleasant spot.' Thus Pat Waddell, one of the eighteen FANYs to form this first ambulance unit, in a rare moment of topographical objectivity. Her first impressions were damp and dismal: 'Amid a deluge of rain, we came to the camp which looked a sorry spectacle with the tents all awry in the hurricane that was blowing.'

Among the eighteen who took over this bracing caravanserai were three future commandants of the Corps: Lilian Franklin, Mary Baxter Ellis and Marian Gamwell. Other notable names among that number were Beryl Hutchinson, who was in the gas attack at Hellfire Corner, and whom we shall come across again at St Omer; Norma Lowson; and Muriel Thompson, one of the first women racing-drivers, for whom the mixed bag of converted private cars – Napiers, Siddeley-Deaseys, a Crossley – must have been a bit of a comedown. There were also two lorries, a big Vulcan and a small Mors box lorry. Later, while the Vulcan was being overhauled, it was replaced by a battered old Wyllis-Overland in which, in May 1917, Pat Waddell tried conclusions with a train on a crossing near the Gare Maritime and lost a leg as a result. A couple of months after the start of the convoy numbers had grown: twenty-two FANYs and two male mechanics, with twelve ambulances, three lorries and a motor-cycle. Of their performance as drivers we have one revealing testimonial, from a sergeant who knew them well. 'When the cars are full of wounded,' he remarked, 'no one could be more patient, considerate or gentle than the FANYs, but when the cars are empty they drive like bats out of hell!'

'When the cars are full of wounded . . .' Day in, day out, and at all hours of the night, the wounded arrived from the front in hospital trains or by barge along the St Omer canal, the barges being reserved for the worst cases since this meant the least jolting. It was the FANYs' job to transfer them either to base hospitals in and around Calais or – this was more likely after a 'push' when every ward was jampacked – on to hospital ships bound for Blighty. Lilian Franklin's report for a typical month sums matters up in her usual dry style: 'During the first fortnight . . . we have carried 985 cases from hospital and barges beside about 160 convalescents to Boulogne.'

A rather fuller picture is supplied by an anonymous contributor to the *Gazette* of September 1916 in an article entitled 'Two Days with the FANY Convoy':

'... then possibly comes the great event of the day – a train down from the front – say at six o'clock the ambulances may be seen lining up on the Convoy road, first the Section Leader with Miss Franklin on her car, then the others, usually in order of seniority, 5, 10, 15, 20 cars, still they come until the end of the line is hidden round the bend of the road, and at the rear comes the Vulcan ...'

The procession winds its way through the town to the Gare Centrale and draws up in the yard, to learn that, as usual, the train is late – but there is a comfortable little *estaminet* with a roaring fire not far away, from which they can see 'the train with its great red crosses' gliding into the platform. The duty medical officers sort out the casualties, 'Miss Franklin and Miss Thompson give the necessary orders to the drivers, the stretcher-bearers start their work and soon the cars begin to creep away ... with their burdens. Such quiet unobtrusive burdens wrapped in brown blankets, with a small brown pillow on a brown stretcher. How much agony and suffering those blankets hide and what tales of heroism could be unfolded ...'

What tales indeed. 'We have just come from a place so terrible,' wrote one of the Australians after the bloody tragedy of Pozières at the end of July, '... a raving lunatic could never imagine the horror of the last thirteen days.' For these men had been brought from the Battle of the Somme, that holocaust in which 60,000 were killed, wounded or missing during the first day.

From the cratered wasteland designated by the immortal names – Thiepval, Contalmaison, La Boiselle, Mametz Wood, Delville Wood – the endless streams of the wounded were led or carried in to the advance dressing stations and forward operating centres, which were soon overwhelmed by sheer numbers, and thence to the casualty clearing stations and the railheads or canal quays for the ninety-mile journey to the Channel ports. For all the care that Lilian Franklin and her team took over loading the men on to their vehicles and driving on poor roads and across bumpy railway lines, many died on the way. Sometimes the men in the back were quiet: the worst was when someone screamed, 'Sister, I can't stand much more of this, drive fast and get it over!' This was the reality of ambulance convoy work.

Simply keeping the vehicles serviceable was a nightmare, particularly in the winter. The anti-freeze provided was useless, and draining radiators, and even carburettors, proved no solution; so at hourly intervals throughout the night the duty drivers had to swing the engines and warm them up. And swinging them was killing work. A backfire broke Marian Gamwell's arm; and often, according to Beryl Hutchinson, the handle would kick you over the mudguard. One girl, cranking away at some brute of a car, was approached by the sergeant. 'Give you a hand, miss?' 'It's all right, thanks,' she replied calmly, 'it usually starts on the 101st swing...' And it did.

'The roads are now in a dreadful condition,' Franklin reported in early 1917. 'The snow has frozen so hard that it is difficult to get a car up the hills, even with the help of chains.' There were other hazards, too, such as 'the narrow escapes owing to the enterprising but inexperienced ladies who are in charge of the Calais trams!' (Does one detect just a hint of professional arrogance there?) Not to mention the hazard of turning on Calais's narrow, crowded quay after taking casualties to a hospital ship. One driver misjudged it and went over the edge into the harbour but was fished out unhurt. As, relatively undamaged, was her vehicle.

The Convoy, like all the FANY units, received fairly regular visits from the top brass – 'Red Flannel' or 'Geraniums' as they termed them. Surgeon-General Woodhouse, who had inspected their last camp before the war, told them that their punctuality and good work 'was making a name for women's work at the front'. Praise, honest and acceptable, but hardly to be compared with that contained in a letter of May 1917 to Mac from General Ditte, Governor of Calais. After noting *les plus grands services* which they had rendered to the town, both as nurses and as drivers, over a period of two years, he continued: '*Elles ont assuré, jour et nuit, avec un dévouement inlassable, le transport des blessés belges, anglais et français et leur prudence comme leur sangfroid a toujours fait l'admiration de tours.*' Somehow, to an English ear at least, compliments sound even more complimentary in French, and the FANYs were showered with them.

During that year, Mac was invalided home with suspected appendicitis, and her beloved brother Bill was killed on the Western Front while trying to rescue a wounded comrade, and was recommended for the VC. Undeterred alike by sickness and sorrow, Mac arranged for eight FANY 'chauffeuses' to be attached to the Belgian Army for ambulance work at the Hôpital de Passage, Gare Centrale, Calais, and was about to start on the French. And where, only a year before, the authorities at home had regarded the idea of women driving in France as totally impracticable, women were taking over in increasing numbers. 'Now that the FANYs have led the way,' Mac could say with justified complacency, 'the VADs are furnishing convoys for all the base towns in France.'

iii

> 'The uncongenial atmosphere of the garage, yard and workshops, the alien companionship of mechanics and chauffeurs ... the ceaseless days and dull monotony of labour will not only rob her of much feminine charm but will instil into her mind bitterness that will eat from her heart all capacity for joy.'
> From an (unnamed) 'leading daily',
> quoted by Pat Waddell

This choice piece of literary garbage, read out in the mess by Pat Waddell, roused her hearers to transports of delight and derision. It all added to the lighter side of life, and no doubt was somehow worked into the repertoire of the concert parties which they put on by request under the banner of the 'FANtastics' or, in reference to that famous remark about 'good red herring', 'The Kippers'. They were able to muster a considerable range of talents: Pat herself had been studying the violin; Beryl Hutchinson had been at drama school; others could play the piano and sing or produce suitable light verse. Sometimes, though there was no ENSA, there would be visiting artistes to reinforce local talent.

There were fairly regular dances; one girl, accused of going to too many, said plaintively that she had only been to ten that month. The records are discreetly reticent on the subject of men, but the strictness of the rules, a few hints here and there, and the slightest exercise of the imagination all suggest that they did not lack male attention: 'pursuitors', as they unkindly dubbed them. In Calais they were only allowed to dine out once a week, and then only in pairs – 'on account of the French', as Pat Waddell tersely puts it – and there were invitations from the various messes round about. One suspects that their escorts were always officers; they were more likely to have horses to loan them, quite apart from anything else. Indeed Mac reveals this incidentally in a sour little aside in one of her letters: 'The WAACs are everywhere and they all go out walks with Tommies. I was very fed up at Abbeville for some Tommies started staring at me and whistling. That will be our trouble now.' At their peak, there were 9000 WAACs in France, but never more than 450 FANYs. The FANYs would always regard themselves as something of an élite.

iv

'But do they not get wounded, these demoiselles?'
'Le Bon Dieu protége ses petites FANYs.'

The end of 1916, the war's halfway point, is a good moment for a brief summing-up. Throughout the year the Corps continued to operate at Lamarck as nurses and drivers and at Camp du Ruchard running the canteen – both for the Belgians – and had at least broken through official resistance to run the Calais Convoy for the British, albeit under the aegis of the British Red Cross Society. Mrs MacDougall had also launched the separate ambulance convoy in Calais for the Belgian Hôpital de Passage, and this was under way in October. It was the best-housed and the best-equipped establishment the FANYs were ever to have, with new vehicles, supplied by the Belgians, comfortable living-quarters, proper workshops, even – ultimate luxury – a washbay. Mac regarded it as 'her' convoy, and used it as her headquarters until the end of the war. But she was often away, and the onus of running it rested on the shoulders of Violet O'Neill Power. The Belgian convoy was to be the centre of a serio-comic confrontation with the BRCS the following year. One of the reasons for Mac's absences was the rumour, circulating that autumn, that Lamarck was to be closed, and she was scouting round for alternative work for the unit.

Apart from these main centres of activity during the first two years of the war, there were a number of temporary assignments which deserve a mention, if only because they illustrate one of the Corps' particular strengths: its compactness of numbers, organization and command gave it the swiftness of response of a flying column.

As early as the end of 1914 members of the Corps were able to find, set up and run a small hospital for convalescent *typhiques* at the urgent request of the Belgians. This was St Ingilvert, between Calais and Boulogne; and for three months it took some of the load off Lamarck. Rather different, but illustrating the same capacity for speed and flexibility, two girls, Doris Russell-Allen and Norah Cluff were seconded to a Belgian field hospital at Hoogstadt, four miles from the front line, for six months of, as they put it, 'cold, wet and rats'. Others took over the running of an emergency canteen at Fontinettes and found themselves having to feed 'two hungry Divisions of our own army'; and, on another occasion, members of the Corps answered a cri de coeur from the YMCA, which had a canteen – known as the Dundee Hut – but not enough people to run it. There were 4000 potential customers 'living under canvas with nowhere to go and nothing to do ... except contemplate a sea of mud'. Margaret Cole-Hamilton – dubbed 'The Sergeant' – and Ida Lewis – 'The Fair Corporal' – soon put that right, with vast quantities of tea, and the inevitable concert.

The NAAFI did not exist – it was started in 1921 – and it was some time before the Expeditionary Force Canteens were set up: the gap was bridged, where it was bridged at all, by the voluntary organizations, YMCA, Toc H – and the FANYs. To the soldiers back from the front, anywhere that provided a cup of tea out of the weather, not to mention a smile from a friendly girl, was a boon indeed.

That word 'voluntary' is important. The Corps was, and remains to this day, just that: in March 1917, it was registered as a Charity under the War Charities Act of the previous year in common with, for example, the BRCS. Far from being paid, members themselves paid a subscription of £1 a year to belong to it, found their own uniforms – as was sometimes all too apparent! – and for all running expenses were dependent on private generosity. To tap which, FANYs on leave were expected to give lectures and talks in their home towns. Money was a constant headache for their Treasurer, Chairman and mentor (part-time), the Reverend William Cluff, and the Secretary at Corps headquarters in Earls Court Road. There, from the outbreak of war until early 1917 the fort was held by Janette Lean, with some part-time help, and thereafter by a succession of other overworked and dedicated women.

Through the Corps office there poured new recruits, relief staff, travel documents, leave, illness, complaints, conditions of service, uniform, and what-not – but also a flood of 'comforts' for which the units were constantly clamouring. Headquarters also handled the accounts: the following are some of the items, taken at random from the second half of 1915:

Total income from subscriptions and donations:	£1568 5s 2d
Cash in bank:	£ 681
Cash in hand:	£ 3 8s 1d
Calais expenses:	£ 436 7s 9½d
'Supplies for abroad':	£ 119 8s 5d
Equipment for Ruchard:	£ 204 17s 3d

In addition to all this, of course, the Secretary was also the honorary editor of the *Gazette*, about 175 copies of which had to be assembled and sent out each month.

By the end of 1916, then, the Corps was well-established in France on both a regular and an ad hoc basis, with fresh opportunities in prospect. But the established organizations, the army, the Red Cross, the Anglo-French Hospital Committee, would never become entirely reconciled to their freebooting ways. As Cluff remarked in a letter to Margaret Cole-Hamilton the following year, 'I cannot make her [MacDougall] understand that the British Military Authorities as well as the British Red Cross Society are very jealous indeed of British women working for Belgian or French even *outside* the area of the BEF, and *within* it they will prohibit it except those units already in existence.'

So, for all the praise – and, indeed, the decorations – showered upon the FANYs on active service in France, there were storms ahead as 1916 faded into the even deadlier year of 1917.

5

The Thunder of the Guns
1917–18

'*The old Priory, with its large airy rooms, its cloisters, and
the huts which have been built to make extra wards, makes
a capital installation for 200 French patients . . . At first
the incessant roar of the cannons was unpleasant . . .*'
Mrs Bernard Allen

Lamarck was closed at the end of October 1916. The Belgians had
built a hut hospital at Port de Gravelines, and the shabby old school –
greatly spruced up since the Corps took it over – was no longer
needed. Needless to say they had a concert and a party – enlivened by
an escapologist from the Army Service Corps who defeated all
attempts by the *gendarmerie* to enchain him – and so ended the first
and most significant chapter of the Corps' active service. Lamarck
had, literally, put them on the map.

But during that autumn Mac had been to see the Société de Secours
aux Blessés Militaires (SSBM) in Paris. Freshly decorated with the
Order of Leopold II for her services to the Belgians, she overcame
French resistance to employing English women, particularly
anywhere near the front, and was given a military hospital twenty
miles from Rheims to run. Its name was Port à Binson, it was a Cister-
cian priory still partly occupied by the Order, and rather like
Lamarck was a hospital more in name than in reality. That is to say,
while the SSBM agreed to supply light, heating, food and doctors, the
Corps had to provide staff for both nursing and transport, medical
equipment – and beds. The airiness with which Mac took on this in-
timidating responsibility caused a furore back at headquarters in

London, and ended in the resignation of the Secretary, Janette Lean.

Nothing illustrates more vividly than Binson the difficulties under which the Corps had to work, or the energy required to overcome them. In a six-week fund-raising blitz through Scotland and the North of England with Mary Baxter Ellis, Mac produced £200 in cash, an assortment of vehicles, a hundred beds, and enough medical instruments and supplies to commission the place. Mrs Allen, quoted at the head of this chapter, and always generous to the FANYs, contributed much of the medical kit; the French Red Cross came up with an X-ray machine, the British with a marquee. 'Thanks to the generosity of friends,' Mac wrote, 'the new hospital has £100 in the local bank.'

Thus equipped, and with a hundred and fifty boxes of assorted gear sent on from Lamarck, the advance party arrived, after numerous vicissitudes, in January 1917. Margaret Cole-Hamilton was in command, and with the other four set to work. In spite of having been a divisional hospital for the previous two years Binson was filthy, with ancient bandages lurking under even more ancient mattresses, and other horrors. Outside the snow fell with a soft persistence and the artillery rumbled like distant thunder. Finally after a month everything was ready; furniture and equipment raised in Britain had been shipped out and arranged; the vehicles were assembled; the Matron, Miss Bullock, arrived. And nothing happened. The previous incumbents had been transferred before they got there, but no new ones arrived.

The first batch – one hundred of them – did not turn up until the end of March, followed by seventy more and by General Descaigne of the Fifth Army, who said all the right things. The two operating theatres were kept busy, and La Prieuré settled into its working routine. Part of it, of course, was still occupied by the *Pères Blancs*; but the two contrasting sets of residents seem to have been able to rub along quite amicably together – at least for most of the time. That summer, however, the Superintendent of the Order issued a mild reproof when the FANYs apparently held what he called *une partie de plaisir* – not quite as louche as it sounds: a tea-party – in the cloisters.

Among their visitors was Mrs Allen, who delivered a dangerous-sounding machine called a de Dion Torpedo, and, in June, Mrs MacDougall, who became positively lyrical. 'The hospital,' she wrote in the *Gazette*, 'is at its best this month with the long windows wide open, and every ward filled with sunshine, fresh air and contented patients. The grounds arc a mass of flowers ... and on every side wooded hills sloping into the distance, and the Marne winding through the picture.' She did not mention the 'incessant roar of the cannons' nor the fact that every now and then one of the contented patients fell into the Marne and drowned.

The work continued steadily all through 1917, and, as a sideline, small relays took over a busy and much-bombed *'Foyer du Soldat'* at Fismes (where they were nicknamed *'les petits soldats'*). Relations between British and French could hardly have been better; and early in January 1918 the head of the SSBM announced plans for the expansion of the hospital, and asked for more nurses to be brought in. A feather in the FANY's cap, it seemed, and Mac went off to recruit the extra staff.

Ten days later Margaret Cole-Hamilton was coolly told that in view of the expansion the SSBM had decided to staff the place with French nurses, so the Corps' services were no longer required, *merci bien!* Coley was furious, regarding it as a slur on a year's honest hard work. The French, it appeared, preferred their wounded to be nursed by their own women, but were not above making use of British women if and when it suited them. The French wounded, however, who were not consulted, preferred, on the whole, to be nursed by the British.

The decision was final; and a month later Coley handed over the keys to a French sister and four nurses and departed, not only from Binson,* but from active service.

ii

'I cannot even now understand how it was she [Mrs Mac-Dougall] incurred the hostility of the British Military Authorities to such an extent that the retention of any unit of the FANY within the area of the BEF became doubtful.'
William Cluff to Cole-Hamilton
(December 18th, 1917)

Before the Binson débâcle, and in pursuit of the apparent entente cordiale, Mac arranged, in the late summer of 1917, for the Corps to

*In her report from Epernay (August 10th, 1918) Doris Russell Allen noted that La Prieuré had been 'quite demolished' during the summer's battles.

take on ambulance work at Amiens. Unfortunately Amiens, fairly close to the front and in a restricted area, also fell within the jurisdiction of British GHQ, and the French had neglected to ask their permission to employ British women. They could not stop them employing FANYs who, outside Calais, acknowledged no master; but they could, and did, require the French to remove them to an area within their own command. The short-lived Amiens unit thus became fragmented, operating at Chateau Thierry in the Aisne, at Bar-le-Duc, at Epernay and Chalons-sur-Marne where we shall return to them in due course.

Meanwhile, the two Calais convoys were in full swing. Lilian Franklin's, known as Unit III* and working for the British, attracted no administrative problems beyond minor skirmishes with the BRCS and the military authorities over such matters as uniform. That a certain 'informality' attended the FANYs' approach to this important subject – as, indeed, it did also to the equally important matter of rank – is apparent from the *Gazette* of October 1916. Janette Lean wrote, 'One costume in particular can only with a stretch of the imagination be called "uniform" at all!' And she went on to describe in detail what should comprise a 'uniform': 'Khaki tunic to have four pockets, FANY buttons and badges, to be made with plain sleeves, a Red Cross circle on each sleeve, the centre of the Cross to be seven inches from the shoulder; bottom of khaki skirt to be ten inches from the ground; khaki puttees and brown shoes or boots or long brown boots to be worn.' The voluminous goatskin coats which many of the girls wore in the winter must have given some of the more pernickety staff officers apoplexy. But uniforms were a subject that inevitably appeared on the agenda from time to time in base towns like Calais: out in the field such details became less important.

Uniform, indeed, came up again in a curious episode involving that other Calais convoy, the one working for the Belgians. At the back of it seems to have been a resentment felt by the BRCS and the military at the FANYs' talent for independent action, a resentment which Cluff attributed to Mac's industrious opportunism. This explains the Amiens incident, and probably lies behind the story that at one point

*Each unit on active service was given a number, but as they were somewhat fluid – Unit I, for example (Lamarck), transferred to Binson when Lamarck closed – it has been thought kinder to spare the reader the confusion in the text.

the BRCS actually moved in on the Belgian Calais Convoy in order to close it down. Mac, having got wind of it in advance, went to the Belgian authorities, who acted with promptitude and decision.

> 'The whole of the Convoy were paraded at the *Etat Majeur*, and there, in the presence of the Base Commandant and Colonel Dieu-Donné, his chief of staff, the FANY members were all weighed, measured, photographed and finger-printed, and sworn in as *Soldats* of the Corps de Transport de Calais (Belge). Blue gorgets, the insignia of the Belgian Corps de Transport, and silver rank badges were issued to the members, and overnight, the FANY Unit V became a fully-fledged unit of the Belgian Army.'*

Thus, when the BRCS arrived, they were 'quietly but firmly reminded that they were . . . "standing on Belgian soil", and that the ladies to whom they referred were Soldats de l'Armée Belge and therefore no concern of the BRCS.'

It is a splendid story; but where it came from is undisclosed, and whether it happened quite like that is doubtful. Dame Irene Ward dates it vaguely as 'in 1917' and connects it with MacDougall being 'in the midst of her plans for Port à Binson' – which had actually been taken over in January of that year. That is neither here nor there; but in December 1917, Mac was writing in the *Gazette*: 'The Belgian convoy will wear Belgian military rank badges on FANY uniform (*they have done this for a year now*).'† Indeed, in October 1916, the month in which the convoy started, it was reported in the *Gazette* that 'members of the Corps are now to be officially attached to the Belgian Army'. But nowhere, neither in the *Gazette* nor in Mac's own letters – long, frequent, and often indiscreet – is there any reference to the theatrical scene between the splendidly named Colonel Dieu-Donné and the representatives of the BRCS. And Mac was not a person to let a good story go to waste.

That there was, during 1917, a showdown over the FANYs' freelance activities is perfectly clear, for in the same passage from the *Gazette* quoted above, Mac continues: 'Any new units (for any army) started in the British area have to be sanctioned by the British Adjutant-General beforehand.' And in the following month, the Adjutant-General issued a stiff injunction on the subject of uniform

FANY Invicta, Irene Ward.
†Author's italics.

and badges of rank. This contained the significant proviso: 'In the case of those units of the FANY Corps working for the Belgians, Officers' rank will be denoted by one or two stars of the Belgian pattern on the lapel of the coat, and NCOs' by stripes on the cuff.' Whatever credence one lends to the Dieu-Donné affair, this seems to be a case of officialdom attempting to salvage its dignity by the belated recognition of a fait accompli. Officialdom had set out to subdue the FANYs and had failed.

The whole affair passed away leaving hardly a ripple; and in any case, the Belgian convoy was far too busy in those months to worry about their puttees. They shifted over 4000 cases in December, and suffered a succession of air raids, with some exceedingly near misses.

iii

'I bore with me chiefly an impression of gaiety, of a set purpose . . . that spiritually works itself out in this determined sticking at the job, this avoidance of any emotion that interferes with it, and in their bodies expresses itself in a disregard for appearances that one would never have thought to find in human woman.'
From 'A personal impression of the FANY camps in France', in Vogue, May 1918

'Do you wash – or do you powder?'
Personal question by a FANY (unnamed) in France

Although 1917 was the year of mud, blood and stagnation on the Western Front, the year of Arras and Paschendaele, military catalepsy did not mean peaceful nights for those in Calais. The Zeppelins had given place to Taubes and Gothas, and in one of these sporadic air raids an 'aerial torpedo' landed in the middle of the camp. But it did not explode. 'We were sure something big had fallen,' Pat Waddell recalled later, 'and yet when we looked there was only a little heap of sand in the middle of the camp which no one seemed to remember having seen before.' After a great deal of digging the monster, six feet long, was laid bare; later, disarmed, it became a much admired trophy in the mess.

On another occasion a German destroyer, so close in that they could smell the cordite, lobbed 150 shells into the town. One demolished the camp cookhouse and another the incinerator – which rather spoilt the rumour that 'the lady drivers had got it proper'.

For them as for everyone else, however, 1918, was going to be very different. While the Amiens convoy was being dispersed along the valley of the Marne, another was being formed to operate at St Omer, twenty-five miles south-east of Calais. It was built around a nucleus of old Calais hands with Muriel Thompson, the former racing driver, in command; it started work towards the end of 1917 under BRCS auspices. Fortunately for the historian one of the founder-members was Beryl Hutchinson, who was the epitome of the FANYs of that war – able, fearless, and bubbling with an ironic, self-deprecating humour – and who put her experiences down on paper.

They arrived, a mixed party of the old hands, new girls and some VAD drivers, to find the town half-inundated. 'The next morning we were on duty and had to meet a train. Sergeant Lowson took over an ambulance with one of the newly arrived drivers as "assistant". The poor girl was told to get the car ready to start for the station while Norma coped with Section A's organization. The report came that it was standing in running water with all four tyres flat. "Get it ready then," said Norma, engrossed with her problems. "Will I give it a wee sweep out?" said a frightened voice and Norma realized that the new entry had to be taught how to change wheels.'

The unit was stationed in a permanent camp on the main road to Arques. It had Nissen huts, a comfortable mess, and a parade ground which served as a vehicle park for the thirty ambulances – at least one of which, a Model T Ford belonging to the Church Army Canteens, had no business to be there. 'The routine,' Beryl Hutchinson goes on, 'was to meet the trains full of wounded and sick men from the Front . . . When they had been sorted out and patched up we took the most serious cases to the barges for a gentle drift down to the coast' – where, of course, the FANY Calais Convoy was waiting for them. 'Then the hospitals were ready for the next load . . . During their 1918 advance the Germans began shelling the town . . .'

That advance, the final, convulsive effort by Ludendorff and his 129 divisions to finish the war, began on March 21st, 1918. Aimed initially at Amiens, it met with immediate success. When it was at last halted, three weeks later, a second thrust was launched, this time at Hazebrouck and Ypres – only ten miles from St Omer – and intended to drive the British back to the sea. That, too, started well for the

Germans – so well that Haig's Order of the Day on April 12th made grim reading: 'With our backs to the wall and believing in the justice of our cause, each one of us must fight to the end.' In three days the German divisions penetrated ten miles, a prodigious distance compared with anything that had been achieved during the previous three years; then they were held, and although they kept up the pressure for another three months, their offensive was spent.

For St Omer, April and May were the toughest months. All the local hospitals were evacuated, which meant that the drivers were running a shuttle service from hospital to train for forty-eight hours non-stop, as well as handling the wounded. Mingling with the ambulances and the retreating soldiers were the refugees, jamming the narrow streets with their carts and prams and pitiful possessions. Twice the girls were told they would have to leave: 'Many high-ranking officers, finding women driving the convoy, ordered us to move out, and we had to explain that we were really too busy.' But they had their own escape plans worked out if the worst happened, and they did allow themselves to be shifted from their rather conspicuous camp to the grounds of a monastery outside the town.

There were numerous air raids during May, culminating in one that lasted for five hours. The girls drove throughout, three of the cars being called to an ammunition dump which had been hit. Altogether for that night's work sixteen Military Medals and two Croix de Guerre were awarded to the FANY and VAD crews. 'All the decorations were questioned,' Beryl Hutchinson notes, 'as there were far too many for one small unit, but each one was so strongly supported for their cool example that in the end all eighteen were allowed.' General Sir Herbert Plumer, GOC Second Army, presented them with their MM ribbons a couple of months later: a proud moment for them, and for the Corps.

When things quietened down a bit, Beryl Hutchinson started organizing Mess Night dances – *parties de plaisir*, it might be thought, though there is no record of the monks objecting – on alternate Saturdays; and, needless to say, being FANYs, they quickly came to terms with the French riding school at St Omer and borrowed their horses four afternoons a week.*

*Hutchinson put what she learnt there from the French Cavalry to good use when she ran her own riding school after the war.

Scenes similar to those in St Omer were taking place that May during the German break-through to the Marne. The following extracts from a report by Doris Russell Allen at Epernay suggest the temper of those hectic weeks:

May 27th/28th:	Called at midnight to go to Bouleuse to evacuate the hospital there as the Germans were approaching... The roads were crowded with refugees, convoys hurrying up reinforcements, stragglers coming back from the line as they were being forced to retreat all the time, wounded men begging to be picked up.
May 29th:	Wounded simply pouring in, in all sorts of conveyances, hundreds waiting to be received – situation appalling – not enough staff to deal with them.
May 30th:	Spent nearly the whole morning evacuating and filling hospitals at the same time.
May 31st:	Evacuated hospitals all day ... an enormous bombardment started ... bombs dropped on the road we had to go along – one dropping near Russell – the horses on the road stampeding and nearly upsetting her car.
June 1st:	Germans getting nearer all the time. This town may have to be evacuated ...

They were moved back to Sézanne, but the work continued.

At Chalons-sur-Marne the story was much the same, and for singular acts of bravery a number of girls were decorated, Fraser, who was wounded, with the Croix de Guerre and the Légion d'Honneur with palm. Then, at last, the moment that had been so long coming:

July 20th:	The news is splendid, and the Hun is being pushed back by the Americans, Italians, French and British. There isn't a German on this side of the Marne now.

The counter-attack mounted by Foch on the Marne had started two days before and marked the beginning of the end. On August 8th the British, French, Australians and Canadians launched theirs from in front of Amiens, and inscribed on the calendar of history 'the black day of the German Army'.

At long last the deadly pattern of trench warfare had been broken. Towards the end of September the Hindenburg Line was breached, and soon Beryl Hutchinson could write: 'The same French Cavalry heralded the change from our normal life, but instead of watching them pass weary and hungry by the light of our one side lamp ... with only the ever-increasing roar of the guns to welcome them, this time they passed in the sunlight with time for a jest with each returning cavalcade of civilians ... It is good to have work, real work again even if the tide of battle has left us behind.'

iv

'How proud we all are of the FANYs who, having stuck to the Belgians so long, through all their adversities, are among the first folk to set foot in reconquered Belgium.'
Beryl Hutchinson in the Gazette, October 1918

Peace, after a long, bad war, is a messy business once the euphoria has evaporated. But first the euphoria. At Chalons 'the town was very lively and we all hung flags on our cars. Very strange to see the town lit up and to go out into bright moonlight without even wondering if there would be an *alerte.*' The church bells rang and the wine flowed, the speeches were delivered, and the compliments; and then, although the war was over and the guns were silent and the aircraft grounded, there was much work still to be done; and, abruptly, everyone was on the move.

The Belgian Corps de Transport had already left Calais in October for Bruges, and the FANY Calais Convoy went with them. On arrival they were mobbed. 'The Grande Place,' Mac wrote in the *Gazette*, 'was one mass of Belgian flags ... and all of a sudden hundreds of people, half-laughing, half-crying, were round the car, clinging to our hands, patting our cheeks, kissing us, sobbing and smiling together.'

From Bruges they went on to Brussels where, there being no ambulance work, they were employed driving Hotchkiss cars for the Belgian War Office and, after long days at the wheel, making the most of comfortable quarters and the gay life of the city. 'Only the necessity of work keeps us from dancing day and night!'

Others had, to begin with at least, a slightly less frivolous time. The Marne units were ordered to Strasbourg, that frontier city of

Alsace, but were held up for a time at Nancy where they were needed. That winter run to the very edge of the old front line and beyond into no man's land revealed the full impact of the war on both the country and the people. In this, its aftermath, the girls became maids-of-all-work, meeting the pathetic trainloads of refugees and *repatriés* (known, for unfathomable reasons, as 'fuggies'), collecting prisoners from internment camps, and picking up forlorn little bands of British prisoners-of-war whom they came across limping, exhausted and lost, along the icy roads – thereby, perhaps, coming closest to fulfilling the purpose for which the Corps had originally been formed.

For most of the girls, as they skidded and slewed their way along the shell-pitted roads and tracks in what had been, not so long ago, the firing-line, this was their first opportunity to see for themselves the trenches and gun emplacements, the ruin and the accumulated rubbish of war. Beneath their eager, appalled curiosity comes an echo of Rawlinson's remark: 'My God, did we send men to fight in this?' And his staff officer's chilling rejoinder: 'It's worse farther on.'

'Of my impressions of the devastated area,' one girl recorded later, 'it is impossible to write, the horror of it haunts me still, but one feeling stands out above all others, and it is an intense admiration for the men who could endure so much and yet keep such wonderful spirits through it all.'

Meanwhile, the tidying up process was already in hand in and around Ypres, and the St Omer unit provided cars and drivers at Poperinghe and Hazebrouck, where parties of men were clearing up shells, unexploded bombs, and all the other debris of the previous four years. The explosives supplied them with a regular stream of accident cases; the conditions of the work-camps a regular stream of sick; and the roads a regular obstacle course. Part of their standard equipment was a number of planks for bridging shell-holes; but it was not always easy to tell those which had only been lightly filled in and into which a car would instantly sink to its axles. None of these hazards deterred Beryl Hutchinson from giving the nurses from the Boulogne hospitals a series of eye-opening tours of the battlefields.

St Omer had already had a friendly visit from King George V back in the summer: now Princess Mary descended upon them, having demanded to see 'those awful FANYs' (Hutchinson's quoted description, not the Princess's) in their natural habitat. Even so she may have been a mite disconcerted to be received by Norma Lowson in pierrot costume, as there was a 'Kipper Concert' about to start. She was regaled with tea and toast and presented with a souvenir in the shape of a little brass box made out of shell-cases and with the FANY badge on it, and on her return to Buckingham Palace declared that her ten days in France and Belgium had been the most exciting in her life.

A rather more formal *partie de plaisir* took place at the Palace of Lacken in Brussels in June 1919. In common with all the other FANY units, the Belgian FANY Convoy had begun to feel that their work was done and it was time to 'leave off our comfortable khaki and get back into the trials of mufti'. Some, indeed, for one reason or another, had gone already: Mac to head for South Africa with her husband, others to get married or attend to neglected family duties. There was to be no forced or formal demobilization, as happened to the regular women's forces; just a general packing-up as each unit came to the end of its useful role. The BRCS had closed down all its convoys at the end of April, and that had, of course, included the Corps' Calais Convoy. Lilian Franklin was awarded the MBE for her stalwart four years' work, and would soon become the Corps' first Commandant. (It was perhaps just as well that Grace MacDougall had resigned, for there was little love lost between them, and it is not easy to imagine her taking second place. 'Such a difficult lady to deal with,' as one harassed Secretary put it.)

But to return to Brussels and June 1919. When it was learnt that the Belgian Convoy was ready to disband, they were summoned to the Palace to be inspected by Her Majesty the Queen of the Belgians. Reeking of petrol – they had all been desperately trying to clean the oil stains off their uniforms – scrubbed and polished, they were lined up in order of seniority, 'the doors were flung open and Her Majesty appeared', and 'Thirty stalwart young Englishwomen gazed curiously at the Queen whose work in the war is the wonder and admiration of women all over the world.' She went down the line, talking to each of them in turn, and then, instead of dismissing them, asked them all to tea. However the unit had come to be *Soldats de l'Armée Belge*, it was a handsome conclusion to their years of service.

For those who survived – and all but one of the FANYs did survive – the ultimate irony of war is that, because it unites the participants in singleness of purpose, it creates a bond between them that is rarely captured in time of peace. That bond is as strong among women as among men.

Two separate but complementary pieces of paper serve to sum up the record of the Corps in the Great War. The first is the tally of decorations awarded to its members – and at their peak there were only 450 of them: 19 Military Medals; 27 Croix de Guerre; 1 Légion d'Honneur; 5 Croix Civique (Belgian), and several other Belgian honours.* In addition, 11 members were mentioned in despatches. In sum, a higher proportion than any other women's formation.

The second comes in a letter to Lilian Franklin from Colonel P. C. H. Gordon of Calais Base. In it he expresses his appreciation to her, to 'Miss Gamwell and the other ladies associated with you' for the 'willing help and loyal co-operation . . . *that converted what was at first an experiment into a triumphant success*'.†

It remains to be seen in the following chapters how durable the esprit de corps engendered by the experiment and its success turned out to be.

*A full list will be found in the Appendix.
†Author's italics.

1914–18

6

Coping with Peace
1919-1939

*'Even if it is small let us be given some task to remind us
that it is a Corps for work and training.'*
Beryl Hutchinson: Gazette (*January 1919*)

*'FANYs are the finest stimulant against Red Tape that the
British Army has ever known.'*
Ibid.

Of one thing the FANYs who congregated at headquarters in May
1919 were determined: the Corps must continue, and not simply as
an old comrades' association, meeting once a year for an evening of
hearty – and gradually fading – nostalgia. In July 1919 the first
annual dinner was held; and three days later twelve FANYs attended a
garden party at Buckingham Palace.

The WRNS and the WAACS (now, under Royal patronage, the
QMAACS) had been summarily demobilized; but no one could demob
the FANYs except themselves, and they had no intention of doing
anything so foolish. So, once again, they were in the position of
having to create a role for the Corps, and at a time when the services –
which did not recognize their existence anyway – were being cut
back, the reaction against everything military was strong, and the
future employment of women in the armed services was unresolved.
'Admitted it is no use learning things if there is no place for us,' Hutchinson wrote in the *Gazette*, 'but it is not much good having
"recognition" if there is nothing to recognize.'

In 1920 Lilian Franklin, who became Commandant in that year,

47

started to explore the possibility of affiliation either with the British Red Cross Society or with the VADs. But as before, affiliation simply did not accord with the FANYs' unshakeable determination to keep their own name, their own uniform, and their own identity. This insistence on the Corps' uniqueness and individuality led later to charges of snobbishness and arrogance; but within the context of the period it was no different from the sense of being members of an élite which was felt by army officers who had been to Sandhurst – or Durham miners who worked down the pit, come to that. In the FANYs' case, however, it was based on the undoubted assumption that any woman who became a FANY was automatically 'officer material'. 'We have the privilege of belonging to the educated classes,' one of them wrote anonymously to the *Gazette*, 'with all the tradition of ruling behind us, and therefore rank as officers *in everyday life*.' They might observe degrees of rank while on duty, as any service must, and did so with a good grace, but off duty they were all birds of a feather. They had their own self-imposed code of conduct: they did not fit easily into the disciplined, stratified hierarchy of a larger organization. And so, for this and other reasons, ideas of affiliation were quietly dropped.

But a deeper reason for the uncertainty of their status in the 1920s was the fact that the War Office simply could not make up its corporate mind as to what kind of women's force it wanted. There was talk of a Women's Army, of a United Women's Corps, of a Queen's Reserve which would be part of the Territorial Army; but none of these materialized, and such women's services as survived the war did so by their own loyalties and efforts. Essentially, apart from the VADs, there were only three: the FANY; the Women's Legion; and the Old Comrades' Association of the QMAAC – all of them voluntary, all destined to be officially ignored until, suddenly, they were needed.

During 1920 the last of the units serving on the continent was dissolved – though a number of FANYs stayed independently to carry on relief work in the long, grim aftermath of the war – and the Corps reverted to its pre-war state of a single cadre, based in London. The faithful William Cluff, adviser spiritual and temporal all through the war years, resigned: so did the Secretary, Andy Anderson, to be replaced by the ebullient Pat Waddell, quite undismayed by having a tin leg. Headquarters moved from Earls Court Road to two upper rooms at 27 Beauchamp Place; and the administration of the Corps was entrusted to a Staff Committee of ten under Franklin's chairmanship. The members, all familiar names, represented the three wartime affiliations, Belgian, British and French – though this would be abandoned later as wartime loyalties weakened. Some familiar names were, however, missing: Mac was in Rhodesia, busy breeding poultry on 9000 acres and producing a baby; Crockett was back in Australia; and Margaret Cole-Hamilton, who had resigned after the Soligny fiasco to serve in the WRAC and the WRAF, only returned to the FANYs later. But Hope Gamwell and Mary Baxter Ellis, both future commandants, were on it, as were Brenda Joynson, Norma Lowson, Cecily Mordaunt, Doris Russell-Allen, Marguerite Moseley, Gwendolyn Peyton-Jones and Edith Walton. The remarkable tenacity of the links between members emerges clearly from the *Gazettes* of those years: from distant corners of the Empire and Commonwealth, from Africa, India, Malaya, Canada, and from less likely spots outside the British connection – the Argentine, Cuba, China – they kept in touch with headquarters and with each other.

The early 1920s were difficult years, all the same, with membership and attendance at camp tending to decline, and a chronic shortage of money: every issue of the *Gazette* contains a plea for members to pay their subscriptions (£1 a year, raised in 1923 to £2), and suggestions as to how funds can be increased. The Corps' greatest asset, undoubtedly, was the relationship it had established and the reputation it had gained with the regular army. Pat Waddell, describing how they picked up their former, peacetime activities – on duty at the Royal Tournament, for instance (a duty taken on occasions by Lady Baird, still armed with her elixir-dispensing hip-flask) – tells of old soldiers recognizing the uniform and yelling 'Good old FANYs!' This reserve of goodwill proved invaluable when in 1921 they set about trying to re-start the annual camps. Brushed off by the War Office, Pat Waddell took herself down to Pirbright and tackled – in her own words – the ripest-looking sergeant-major with a chest full of medals she could find; and, having established the fact that he knew the FANYs and even remembered the pre-war camps, was able to wheedle out of him all the gear they needed. By such a ruthless application of charm and the power of precedent the girls not only succeeded in setting up their first post-war camp in 1921, but managed to get themselves attached to the MT Workshops at Aldershot with the object of achieving regular standards in driving and mechanics. A pleasant story illustrates the success of this process of infiltration. The officer commanding the Guards Brigade rode into their camp one day to find his signallers, his band instruments, and one of his limbers all there. 'Well, you'll let me have the Brigade back when you've finished with it, won't you?' he remarked with tolerant irony.

Such tolerance, expanded into active help from officers commanding down – one sergeant in the RAMC actually gave up his leave in order to give them lectures and training – can only have stemmed from the Corps' outstanding wartime record and the palpable enthusiasm and seriousness of purpose of its members.

Not all, however, was sweetness and light. Among the sixty young women who attended that first camp were quite a few new recruits who did not know what they were in for, and were fairly shaken when they found out. 'These two weeks,' Franklin – who showed a tendency to refer to Aldershot as Boulogne and demanded the discipline and smartness of active service – told them on arrival, 'these two weeks are to be devoted to work'; thereby echoing Mac's words of eleven years before, and shivering the timbers of some of her more naive listeners.

The spirit and enthusiasm of the old hands were not enough, all the same, to prevent a steady decline in numbers over the next three years. Attempts to strengthen the Corps by other means were equally fruitless. In 1923, for instance, Franklin attended a meeting with Dame Katherine Furse, former Chairman of the Joint Women's VAD Committee, and Dame Helen Gwynne-Vaughan, former Director of both the WAAC and the WAAF – a formidable lady of whom we shall hear more later – with the idea of turning the FANY into a kind of officers training corps to supply any or all of the women's services which might be created. As at that time there were none, nor would there be for another fifteen years, the idea was stillborn. In the same way, an attempt to reform the structure of the Corps itself failed to strengthen its support. A combination of post-war reaction, a lack of clear purpose, and a discrepancy between old and new, active and inactive members sapped its support. At the 1925 camp a mere twenty-seven turned up, and the *Gazette* commented morosely, 'The numbers were so small it hardly seemed worth going on.'

Nor might it have been had it not been for two, quite different, events which mark 1926 as an important year in the annals of the Corps.

1. Captain Baker (left), Lilian Franklin and Sir Francis Vane of the League of Imperial Frontiersmen, on horseback.

2. The First HQ: Grace Ashley Smith (with dog) and three other F.A.N.Y.s on the roof of Gamage's department store in Oxford Street, c. 1911. They were teased by passers-by in the street below.

3. Bourne End Camp, 1912; a first aid convoy led by Lilian Franklin.

4. The French convoy waiting to leave London.

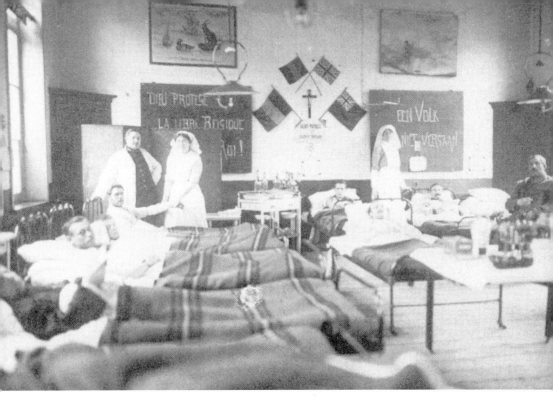

5. 'Dear dirty old Lamarck...'

6. Muriel Thompson CG (left) with F.A.N.Y. drivers.

7. Sadie Bonnell receiving the Military Medal from General Plumer, France 1917.

8. The 1924 F.A.N.Y. camp. Demonstration of a portable transceiver at a time when the Corps was making its first forays into communications, a skill that would prove invaluable during the Second World War.

9. The 1932 F.A.N.Y. camp. A combined gas drill/First Aid exercise.

10. The 1937 F.A.N.Y. camp: vehicle maintenance, a skill still practised by the Corps
    – though not in service dress!

11. Inspection in East Africa of the Kenya section of the W.T.S., the first of any recognized women's auxiliary unit to be authorized and trained outside Great Britain, 1938.

12. A lecture in progress; it may have been anything from encryption to recognition of arms

13. Vehicle maintenance, this time "for real".

14. A "scramble" at 2 M.T.T.C., Camberley.

15. Members of the F.A.N.Y. motor cycle unit.

16. "The most valuable link in the whole chain of our operations..." Wireless operators with Special Operations Executive.

17. Princess Elizabeth, now HM The Queen, being watched with maternal interest by Queen Elizabeth, training at Camberley with the A.T.S. in 1944.

18. F.A.N.Y. BRCS ambulances crossing a Bailey bridge. There were 200 members in this unit.

19. Odette Churchill,
    GC, MBE, L d' H,
    after the war.

20. Three of those who were murdered *(left to right)*: Yolande Beekman, C. de G.,
    Violette Szabo, GC, and Andrée Borrel, Medaille de la Resistance.

21. ...and two who survived, Eileen Nearne, MBE, C de G, and Yvonne Baseden,
    MBE, C de G.

 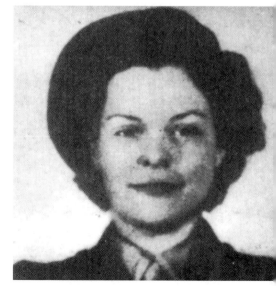

F.A.N.Y./SOE Agents in the Second World War.

22. The Corps took its rightful place in the Victory Parade.

23. F.A.N.Y. mobile library, Hong Kong. Between 1945 and 1947, the Far East Welfare Unit had 400 Corps members.

24. F.A.N.Y. contingent at the Lord Mayor's Show in the City of London, early 1950s.

25. The City of London Police casualty bureau on call-out following the Moorgate underground crash, 1975.

26. Planning an exercise.

27. Orienteering on a combined unit exercise in the 1980s.

28. F.A.N.Ys practice on an army shooting range.
29. Commandant Anna Whitehead, OBE *(right)* CO 1990–1997, with her successor,
Lynda Rose.

30. Mme Villameur (Lise de Baissac) with six F.A.N.Y. parachutistes, Instructors from ETAP at PAU, and personnel from the military airbase at Orléans-Bricy, France 2002.

31. Three members of F.A.N.Y. on exercise with Instructor from 70 (Essex Yeomanry) Squadron, 71 Signal Regiment: France 2002.

32. HRH The Princess Royal, Commandant-in-Chief, F.A.N.Y., (Princess Royal's Volunteer Corps).

ii

'*The Corps has shown very clearly that it does not approve of democratic government.*'

Gazette: March 1926

'*Constitutional Government is being attacked . . . Stand behind the Government . . . The laws are in your keeping . . .*'

Stanley Baldwin, May 3rd, 1926

The only link between these two quotations is that, in their quite separate ways, they signalled the FANYs' escape from the doldrums of the immediate post-war years. The first, from the *Gazette* editorial of March 1926, refers to the promulgation of the new Corps Constitution, agreed at a general meeting six months before, by which the Headquarters Committee was abolished, and its powers vested in the Commanding Officer, Lilian Franklin. The instigator of the change was Marian Gamwell, the younger of those two intrepid★ sisters who had provided the 'Motor Bath' of fragrant memory.

Under the new system, the CO was to appoint a Regimental Board of five – Second in Command, Adjutant and Treasurer *ex officio* and two others – with whose help and advice she would manage the Corps. In addition there was to be an Advisory Council, composed of the Honorary Colonel-in-Chief and four others normally drawn from the Corps' list of Patrons, to act as the ultimate arbiter in its affairs. This administrative structure, introduced after a referendum among all serving FANYs,† remains in force today. Other changes included the introduction of an Active and a Reserve list to resolve the problem of seniority versus participation; and, more significant, a change of title. As General Sir Evan Carter pointed out at the meeting at which the new constitution was introduced, both 'Nursing' and 'Yeomanry' had become out of date: an apter title would be Ambulance Car Corps (FANY). This was duly adopted, but like other attempts along the same lines, made no difference in practice. FANYs they were, and FANYs they would remain.

★The word 'intrepid' is not used lightly: Marian and Hope Gamwell, in between energizing the FANY, had gone to East Africa and literally hacked a farm out of virgin land in the Rhodesian Highlands. Their adventures are described in an unpublished book which is in the FANY library.
†Though only 72 out of the 126 members voted: 66 for, 6 against.

And now at last, after seven years of precarious existence, during which the question 'What is it all for?' continued to crop up, an answer of sorts appeared. With the social and economic causes underlying the General Strike of May 1926 we are barely concerned here, though it is worth putting it briefly into its historical context. At the root of it was the state of the coal industry. The slump immediately after the war was followed by a short-lived boom and a further slump; and with each recession the mine-owners attempted to meet it by cutting wages and increasing hours. No policy could have been better calculated to unite the Trade Union movement, first against the employers, later, when Baldwin was seen to range himself with them, against the Government itself. Thus was born the Triple Alliance of miners, railwaymen and transport workers which, for nine days in 1926, brought the country to a halt.

The lines of battle had been drawn, on the Government side in the Emergency Powers Act of 1920, and in the emergency road transport system worked out at the same time and quietly kept on file during subsequent years. It was brought to a state of readiness towards the end of 1925: indeed, the FANYs were warned that autumn that they might be needed. And on May 1st, 1926, Franklin was summoned to the War Office and told to provide twenty private cars and drivers for transport duties as required, from Monday morning.

The strike began officially at midnight on Monday, May 3rd. During the day nearly a hundred members of the Corps reported to Headquarters for a variety of duties: ferrying War Office staff to and from their homes; taking over ambulances in London and at Aldershot; taking the Duty Medical Officer on his rounds; or, rather more interestingly, escorting the night food convoys on their regular run from Aldershot to the London docks and back.

There were sporadic outbreaks of violence, spontaneous or provoked, but for the most part the peculiarly British attitude towards such social upheavals – tolerant, wry, resigned – prevailed; and the FANYs, in common with the retired army officers in boiler suits living out their boyhood fantasies on the footplate, the undergraduates in plus-fours turning out as signalmen or porters, went on their way, mocked but unmolested. On occasions the FANYs were mistaken for WAACs who, it was assumed, had been called up for the 'Emergency' – insult rather than injury.

After nine days, the Trades Union Council agreed to call off the strike – though the miners rejected the terms with resolute fury; not until the end of November, seven months later, did they finally return to the pits. The Government – and the mine-owners – had the unconditional surrender they wanted: but at a price which is still being paid today.

For the FANYs, the results of the General Strike were, if disproportionate to their part in it, more agreeable. They had been the only women's corps officially employed by the War Office, and the War Office was duly grateful. Letters of appreciation came quite quickly, praising their 'public spirit' and 'zealous help under trying circumstances'; but for the one accolade they wanted, recognition by the Army Council, they had to wait rather longer.

Franklin had quickly seized the opportunity presented by that 'special relationship' with the army during the strike to write to the Army Council. Enclosing a copy of the new Constitution, she offered the Corps' services to the War Office for transport duties in a national emergency, at home or abroad, on a permanent basis. If the offer was accepted, she suggested that it should be made official by an announcement in Army Orders, and by inclusion in the monthly Army List. General Carter, the Corps' Honorary Colonel, supported the request; and in due course Army Order No 94 appeared in the Army List of April 14th, 1927:

'The First Aid Nursing Yeomanry (Ambulance Car Corps) has been officially recognized by the Army Council as a voluntary reserve transport unit. The Corps has placed its services at the disposal of the War Office for service in any national emergency *either as a unit, or, in the event of a Woman's Reserve being organized, as individual members of that reserve.** The Corps will receive no financial assistance from the Army funds.'

'Probably,' commented the *Gazette* editorial in July 1927 in which the announcement appeared, 'the prompt response of the Corps to the call for volunteers last year, and the excellent work that was done during the Strike, influenced the decision of the Army Council to afford us the official recognition.' But the editorial did not comment on the proviso italicized here. This central article of FANY faith – the

*Author's italics.

Corps' uniqueness and independence – even if, as in the discussions with Furse and Gwynne-Vaughan in 1923, it was realized that it might have to be modified in the interests of survival – was to come under intolerable pressure later on. In the euphoria engendered by Army Order No 94, the future implications of that proviso were perhaps not fully appreciated.

A second bonus to come out of the strike was a steady rise in recruitment. This led in turn to the formation of small sections away from London, starting with Northumberland and Hampshire in 1928 and followed by others in Leicester, Glasgow and Yorkshire in the early 1930s, and also one, under Lady Sidney Farrar, in Kenya. Both enthusiasm and persistence were needed to put these local sections together, and induce members, often widely scattered, to attend. Beryl Hutchinson, running her livery stables (on Belgian Cavalry lines) in the New Forest, talks of 'a drive of fifty miles or so, or a long and tedious cross-country train journey' for many of them: at the same time the FANYs, with their strong county connections and well-tempered determination, were often able to enlist the support of Territorial Associations for training, and local bigwigs as patrons.

The numbers attending the summer camps reflected this renewed interest in the Corps. The handful of 1925 had doubled the following year, with eleven new recruits and seven old hands who had rejoined; and this trend continued until, in 1939, one camp site could no longer accommodate them all and they had to split up between three separate ones. By 1926, however, the Corps was already providing its own instruction in all but the most recondite ailments of the motor vehicle, and thirty-five of those present took and passed the relevant Army tests for driver-mechanic. Promotion, too, was properly organized: troopers wishing to become lance-corporals not only had to pass exams in first aid, map-reading, mechanics, drill and gas, but had to produce a meal for the assembled company. As an echo of direr days, the course for the driving test was laid out on the lines of the dreaded quay at Calais – but without the Calais penalty for an error of judgement.

Increasingly, during the inter-war years, the role of the Corps shifted away from the combination of nursing and transport to primarily transport, and thus its closest links were with the Service Corps; and by 1928 the training of FANY officers and NCOs in mechanics and driving was directly matched to RASC practice.

Unpaid and unsubsidized they might be, but they now felt much more 'official' than ever before. They had been granted, however guardedly, official recognition; and in their Honorary Colonels – General Sir Evan Carter from 1922 until his death eleven years later, and his successor, Major-General Sir Evan Gibb, Colonel Commandant of the RASC – they had powerful support where it was most needed. Significantly, military administration and law, and history of the Army, were included in the training syllabus; a clear indication of the increasing 'professionalism' of the Corps' outlook.

With each successive year their links with the Army became firmer and more relaxed. Their annual presence at Pirbright was taken for granted, and the loan of tents and gear – even rising to 'a Club Tent with easy chairs, lamps, coloured ashtrays and array of illustrated papers' – was made without demur. However, in case the reader should be anxious that the Corps was getting soft, let it be said that the training was becoming more elaborate and testing. Night convoy driving was enlivened by 'gas alerts' and threats of 'enemy observation'; normal driving by the introduction of a six-wheeled ambulance, and an interesting cross-country course of 1 in 3 gradients with plenty of gorse and bracken to be negotiated. Camps usually ended with a special demonstration: on one occasion an exhibition of drill, but carried out in Baby Austins. 'The little cars fell in on the marker, numbered, formed fours, marched and formed squad, ending by a triumphant March Past when on the command "Eyes Right" a roar of horns went up in salute.' There was also, in the FANY tradition, an entertainment. This took the form one year of everyone turning up in their interpretation of the original Corps mess-kit, which has been described as 'the first and still the most elegant feminine mess uniform on record. A fashionable white muslin dress was topped by a short scarlet bolero, trimmed with pale blue at neckline and cuffs and with fine frogging across the front.'[*] 'It's true they wore their monkey jacket . . .' a report reads, 'but – shades of 1914 – they disdained the muslin and substituted azure blue satin shorts.' And as if this weren't saucy enough, the show ended with a ballet, 'The CO's Parade' in which Boss Franklin of all people 'was represented in a tunic over a short pale rose ballet skirt with a wreath of olive leaves in her hair'. Pirbright in July was by no means all gas masks and grease-guns.

[*]Elizabeth Ewing, op. cit.

7

The Shotgun Wedding
1932–1939

'An Official letter was sent to all members of the Corps
... informing them that Her Royal Highness Princess
Alice, Countess of Athlone, has done the Corps the great
honour of becoming its President.'
                                Gazette, September 1933

The early 1930s were good years for the Corps. Numbers rose
steadily; camps were well-attended; the range of skills was extended,
the standards acquired were raised. (In parenthesis, the first woman
member of the Institution of Engineers and sometime President of
the Women's Engineering Society, Verena Holmes, BSc (Eng),
AMIMechE, MInst Met, was an ex-FANY from Lamarck.) And such
remarks from an inspecting General as 'I have always looked on the
FANYs as the women's equivalent of the Brigade of Guards and as
regular army' did nothing to diminish their sense of being a *corps
d'élite*. In September 1930 Headquarters moved once again, this time
from Beauchamp Place to 'beautiful new offices' – provided through
the courtesy of the Council of the BRCS – at 14 Grosvenor Crescent.

In 1932 Lilian Franklin, 'Boss' to a whole generation of FANYs and,
for ten years, Commandant, resigned, to be succeeded by Mary
Baxter Ellis, the tall, immensely capable Northumbrian who had
joined during the war. Franklin, dour, dedicated, unflappable, had
been the ideal counterweight in the early days to the no less dedicated, far from dour, unstoppable Mac. But it was Franklin who had
nurtured the Corps through the difficult and discouraging post-war
years, and who had been responsible for giving it an administrative
structure of lasting validity. Under her wise leadership the FANYs had

discovered, out of the fantasies of their founder and the hard and varied experience of the war, a role that fitted their particular abilities and circumstances; and this had achieved official recognition. Much was to change during the coming years, but the foundations laid during her years as Commandant proved earthquake-proof. Baxter Ellis summed up the central FANY faith when she took over: she saw their worth 'not only as a training for war or civil strife, but for individual characters and the ideals they pursued'.

Even more important for Corps morale than recognition by the army was the appointment, in May 1933, of HRH Princess Alice, Countess of Athlone, as President. The first, tentative approach had been made to King George V over a year before: that the request for a royal president* should have been granted was a real feather in the FANYs' cap, and had considerable practical importance as well. Princess Alice made the Corps her own, attending the meetings of the Advisory Council, inspecting the annual camps, and displaying an endearing tendency, when addressing the girls, to say 'We ...' – not the royal 'we', but 'we, the Fanys ...' And, of course, simply by being President she gave the Corps a cachet that was even more significant in the 1930s than it is today. Royal patronage brought another, less obvious advantage: it reassured those anxious mothers whose daughters wanted to join the FANYs. 'If dear Princess Alice is president, they must be quite respectable ...' And this in turn helped recruitment.

ii

'We are a transport unit, and people, especially officials, must be able to recognize us as such.'
M. Baxter Ellis, 1937

'Unless the strength of the Corps is considerably increased both in London and the counties, they cannot be officially depended upon in the opening phases of war.'
Princess Alice, 1937

One outlet for their energies which the FANYs exploited from 1934 onwards was Voluntary Driving 'for hospitals and other approved

*The current Commandant-in-Chief is Princess Anne.

schemes of social service', backing up the regular ambulance service or providing transport, on both a routine and an emergency basis, where none existed. A special category of Reserve B members for volunteers who were not regular FANYs was instituted, though anyone volunteering to join the scheme was encouraged to transfer to the Active List. They used their own cars, supplied their own petrol, and helped to fill a gap in the somewhat sketchy welfare pattern of the time. Although they were to be 'carefully examined and tested in their driving and knowledge of Road and Traffic regulations', there is no mention of first aid as being a necessary qualification.

Although training in first aid continued as part of the normal curriculum throughout these years and as early as 1922 the Corps had two doctors, Ince and Ebden, the emphasis was shifting more and more towards transport in its various guises. This had been recognized by the attempt, in 1926, to change the Corps title by adding Ambulance Car Corps, and relegating FANY to a mere parenthesis; but apart from its appearance in Army Orders, it seems to have disappeared without trace or regret. 'Not once but many times,' Baxter Ellis said in 1937, 'has this sore subject been discussed. Each time the old sentiment has won.' But she went on: 'As a mechanical transport unit it [the title FANY] has actually come to hamper us, entailing endless explanations, and in some cases even refusal of certain important points of training or possible work or help from the authorities. A First Aid Unit is tied to a type of work which the Corps ceased to undertake actually in 1918, and finally in their official agreement with the War Office.' So, duly, the First Aid Nursing Yeomanry became the Women's Transport Service (FANY) which it remained until 1999.

But as a later Commanding Officer, Mrs Sheila Parkinson, admitted, answer any telephone caller with 'Women's Transport Service', and they say '*Who*?' Say 'The FANYs' and they know at once. For whatever else he did or did not achieve, Sergeant-Major Baker hit upon a title for his nurses on horseback that provided them with a friendly, memorable and inexpungable acronym.

Almost as important as the change of title, and simultaneous with it, was the expansion of the 'establishment' – in army terminology, the actual or presumed strength of a formation and the ratio of officers of various ranks and NCOs appropriate to that strength. Thus the establishment of the FANY was laid down in 1926 (slightly revised seven years later) on a presumed strength of between 400 and 500, which meant that there was only one officer with the rank of captain: the Second-in-Command. Prospects of promotion were correspondingly lean through the scale. 'But now,' Baxter Ellis wrote in the *Gazette* in June 1937, 'thanks to our recruits, as well as the great expansion of our aims and possible work, this old establishment is too limited . . .'

Under the revised plan, the establishment was to be based on a hypothetical strength of 800, divided into a number of Groups of two Sections of 50 members. Corps Headquarters with its staff was also to be a Group, working directly under the Commanding Officer and responsible for the administration of the whole Corps through individual and largely autonomous Group Headquarters. Any single section would start to take on the characteristics of a Group as soon as it was past the 50 mark. 'I think you will all realize,' Baxter Ellis concluded, 'the very much wider opportunities for training in actual administration and executive work which this new arrangement will give.' Finally, the Second-in-Command was to become Assistant Commandant, with a rank higher than captain, but without any *automatic* right of succession.

Within eighteen months of these important changes, however, there seemed to be a real danger that the Corps, name and all, would be wiped out.

iii

'*I am to explain that the Department agrees that the entity of the Women's Transport Service will be retained and that the Headquarters of the Women's Transport Service will continue to be recognized by the War Office.*'
Letter, September 20th, 1938, from War Office to Sir Geoffrey Lawrence, Chairman of the FANY Advisory Council

'*As events turned out, no one would question that the original decision to serve Army Transport by the WTS (FANY) was impossible of fulfilment.*'
Irene Ward, FANY Invicta

The origins of the threat to the FANY as an independent entity may be traced back to those insubstantial plans for a 'Women's Army' which were mentioned in the previous chapter. It was perfectly obvious to anyone who had been closely involved with the demands made on women during the Great War that if war should occur again, women would be just as urgently needed as they had been then. It was simply another case of Kipling's *Tommy*:

'Oh, it's Tommy this, an' Tommy that, an' "Tommy, go away";
But it's "Thank you, Mister Atkins," when the band begins to play.'

Alone among the women's services, the FANYs refused to 'go away' but quietly continued to train and grow throughout the 1920s and '30s. In 1934, however, two outstanding women, Circe Lady Londonderry, the founder of the Women's Legion, and Helen Gwynne-Vaughan, joined forces to try and create a new and enlarged Women's Legion composed of the remnants of the Legion itself, the VADs and the FANY.

As Shelford Bidwell remarks:* 'The campaign for the creation of a women's service was long, its manoeuvres involved, and it was fought in many a committee and conference and with many a telephone call and at many a luncheon and dinner table.' For all that, the Women's Legion defied revival: instead, something entitled the Emergency Service was formed, initially to provide officers for the Legion (if it ever got off the ground), then simply to provide officers for whatever women's service finally materialized – a project that Franklin and Gwynne-Vaughan had discussed for the FANY back in 1923. Meanwhile the FANYs went on their way unperturbed.

By now it was 1937. Italy had invaded Abyssinia; Germany had reoccupied the Rhineland; both were using the Spanish Civil War as a training-ground; and Britain, while hoping for peace, was reluctantly preparing for war. Once more the chimera of an all-purpose, all-embracing service, created round the nucleus of the Emergency Service, the surviving remnants of the Women's Legion – its Motor Transport Companies – and the FANY, made its appearance; and Mary Baxter Ellis was invited to command it. On the advice of Sir Evan Gibb and the Advisory Council, she declined. Once more, the file went back into the pending tray.

*In *The Women's Royal Army Corps.*

But the drift towards war was acquiring an irreversible momentum, and among the belated preparations for it was an altogether more purposeful scheme for a women's service. The new service, envisaged as supplying drivers, clerks and cooks for both the Army and the RAF – but not the Navy – was to be complementary to the Territorial Army but, for various doctrinal military reasons, not part of it. It was hastily cobbled together and the FANYs were told, in effect, that if they did not join there would be no job for them in the event of war. They did succeed in extracting an assurance that they would be able to retain their identity within the larger organization – as the letter quoted at the head of this section makes clear – and, on the strength of the promise and under pressure of the threat, they agreed to participate. But even before the promise had been put into writing, indeed on September 9th, 1938, the Auxiliary Territorial Service (ATS) was established by Royal Warrant: 'an organization', to quote, 'whereby certain non-combatant duties in connection with our military and air forces may from time to time be performed by women'. On the 21st the FANY, in common with the Motor Transport Companies of the Women's Legion and the Emergency Service duly, if reluctantly, signed an agreement with the ATS. From that moment on an overwhelming proportion of FANYs, including their Commandant, became members of the Motor Driver Companies (Army), Auxiliary Territorial Service, and would be increasingly subjected to the discomfort of a dual loyalty.

iv

'*The FANY preferred, regardless of any agreements, gentlemen's or otherwise, to go on in their own way for the excellent reason that they felt they knew what they were doing while the newly appointed (ATS) commandants at that stage of affairs were frankly beginners.*'
Shelford Bidwell

The agreement with the War Office which Mary Baxter Ellis and Lady Hailsham – who had joined the Advisory Board in 1933 and become Honorary Treasurer the following year – signed on September 21st, 1938, allocated to each of the three voluntary organizations their separate responsibilities. The FANY undertook 'to assist the TA

Associations in raising all motor driving companies of 150 each (approximately) required for service with the Army' – that is to say, 1500 driver-mechanics, since there were to be ten companies covering virtually the whole country, including Scotland and Northern Ireland. The Mechanical Transport Section of the Women's Legion would do roughly the same for the RAF; the Legion itself was to provide clerical and administrative staff; and the Emergency Service would undertake officer training. At the same time – and this is the vital point – the parent organization into which eventually these component units were to be fitted was itself still little more than an embryo. The ATS, which three years later would have a strength of over 200,000, engaged in virtually every non-combatant trade from tinsmith to ammunition officer, from cooking to weapon-testing, and which would be the spiritual and physical home of the majority of FANYs for the duration, was born feet first, and with those extremities in very much better shape than the rest of it. A certain lack of co-ordination during the first months of life was inevitable.

Once again, Pat Waddell's remark about the preparedness of the FANYs applied: within a matter of weeks they produced a thousand driver-mechanics, launched a recruiting drive for a further five hundred, and started an officers' and NCOs' training-course at Camberley. Never was the foresight of the Corps' senior members in keeping the FANY in being in the dogdays after the Armistice, nor Baxter Ellis's reorganization twenty years later, more fully justified than in that hurly-burly of headlong enlistment and undirected activity. Bidwell writes of 'a great many hastily-recruited ATS officers [who] had had no time to discover how the army worked, what they were supposed to do, or even how to obtain what they wanted': in contrast, in 1938 there already existed a well-trained cadre of 400–500 FANYs who knew all these things, thanks to their regular training programmes and their close liaison with the very heart of the army at Aldershot. 'Tony' Kingston-Walker, Second-in-Command to Baxter Ellis, mentions 'the way these Generals talked to them like normal regimental officers, teaching them their job in casual conversation . . . All of which built up the Corps' savoir faire and ability to cope with many strange situations later in their army career.'

Until Dame Helen Gwynne-Vaughan took command of the ATS in July 1939, and for an increasingly uneasy year thereafter, the FANYs continued to run their own affairs in the old way. Their Motor Driver

Companies, a self-governing entity within the evolving structure of the ATS, remained under the jurisdiction of Headquarters – which, early in 1939, moved from Grosvenor Crescent to larger premises in Ranelagh House, 10 Lower Grosvenor Place – kept their own uniform, and, to the growing disapproval of the younger, rank-conscious service, followed their own relaxed custom of easy-going sorority between commissioned and non-commissioned off duty. Such a position of independence was to become less and less tenable and the new service, under the lash of its Director's thrusting personality, began to assume the more rigid attitudes of a regular army formation. A final clash was inevitable from the beginning, and intimations of it were becoming apparent as early as October 1938 when Gwynne-Vaughan, at that time merely commandant of her own Emergency Service, first 'invited' FANY officers to attend her Officer School of Instruction, and then laid down that they *must* attend in order to qualify as officers in the ATS. This did not go down well with the FANYS.

Much has been made of the scrapping of the original agreement by which the Corps was to retain its identity within the ATS, and the substitution of a completely different one by which it was completely absorbed, and the matter was undoubtedly handled maladroitly by the War Office. But even Dame Irene Ward, who damns it roundly,* is forced to admit that: 'Looked at dispassionately . . . it can be easily understood how unwieldy and impossible it would have been to maintain a separately controlled body within a large military organization during a war.'

The gradual erosion of the FANY–ATS's status as FANYs was extended over almost three years, and although the *coup de grâce* did not take place until June 1941 – when the ATS became subject to the Army Act† – and thus takes us beyond the chronological bounds of the present chapter, it is convenient to summarize it here.

Until the outbreak of war in September 1939 the Motor Driver Companies scattered from Devon to the Highlands of Scotland, and corresponding roughly with the old Sections, carried out the duties allocated to them by the ATS, but still owed their final allegiance to FANY Headquarters. And that was the rub, as far as the Director of

*FANY Invicta.
†Army Council Instruction, June 6th, 1941, under Regulation 6 of the Defence (Women's Forces) Regulations, 1941; and Order in Council, May 30th, 1941.

ATS was concerned. She made one peremptory attempt to close it down by equating it with the Territorial County Units, stating in a letter to the Advisory Council at the end of August: 'Once the Companies are at their war stations, the present Headquarters ... will cease to exist.' But FANY Headquarters was in no way equivalent to TA Units Headquarters: it was private property, paid for and run by the FANYs out of FANY funds, and could not be disposed of so easily. Three months later, in December 1939, a more drastic gambit was tried. The London-based Motor Companies were instructed by the War Office to set up a Driver Training Centre at Camberley, and take their headquarters with them. So thither Baxter Ellis went, becoming its Commandant and also Inspector of Motor Companies (ATS), and urgently summoning Marian Gamwell home from Northern Rhodesia to hold the fort in Ranelagh House. For there were still FANYs who were not in any of the Motor Companies and thus still independent of the ATS and its Director. They dubbed themselves the 'Free FANYs'; and the story of the Corps' renascence through them forms, in all its colour, variety and tragedy, the other main strand in the FANYs' contribution to the war-effort. The Motor Companies of the FANY–ATS did sterling work, as we shall see; but the clear, independent spirit of FANYdom burnt brightest in those who remained outside. The FANY–ATS might be allowed, as a special concession, to wear a FANY flash on the shoulder of their ATS uniforms: the Free FANYs wore their own uniform as of right. Their links with their shanghaied sisters were now sentimental, for they no longer had any authority over them. To that extent Dame Helen Gwynne-Vaughan, Director ATS – though not for much longer – had got her own way.

For the moment, however, we are back in September 1938, in the curious period of slightly guilty relief that followed Neville Chamberlain's meeting with Hitler. The FANYs may have been well-organized, but a rapid trebling of their numbers taxed the Corps' human and material resources to their limits.

Abroad, the one and only FANY Section – in Kenya – was training hard under the leadership of Lady Sidney Farrar, who also found time to become the first Woman Member of the Legislative Council; and at home Headquarters found time to decorate and furnish part of the new premises as a Regimental Club, open to both FANYs and members of the ATS.

And so, after a year's grace, on September 3rd, 1939, that same lugubrious voice that had declared 'peace in our time' now informed the country that we were at war with Germany.

1919–36

8

FANYs in Chains
1939–1945

'*Baxter Ellis reported that the position of the Motor Companies had become intolerable. The original Agreement had not been kept and she had been constantly harassed by the threat to abolish the Headquarters of the Motor Companies.*'
Advisory Council Minutes, April 1st, 1940

'*. . . any agreement made between the Army Council and any other body could and would be altered, if it was thought wise or necessary to do so.*'
Statement by the Adjutant-General, ibid.

The Auxiliary Territorial Service was the collateral descendant of the WAAC which, in common with the WAAF and the WRNS, had been scrapped soon after the Armistice. A much younger Gwynne-Vaughan had been the WAAC's Deputy Controller in 1917. The ATS itself would, after World War II, revert to the original title – with, thanks to Queen Mary's patronage, the addition of 'Royal'. In each of these manifestations its members were restricted to non-combatant duties, and although this led to some nice ethical problems – in, for instance, their employment in anti-aircraft batteries where the distinction between loading and actually firing a gun became so subtle as to be virtually invisible – it forbade them to carry or use small arms.* This was one of the reasons why no ATS members became SOE agents: the FANY suffered no such limitations.

---

*Members of the present-day WRAAC do learn to handle and fire such weapons.

No one, least of all Gwynne-Vaughan herself,* has put forward a valid reason for her vendetta against the FANY. Marian Gamwell said that 'she was the most tactless person I think I have ever had the misfortune to know'; and Baxter Ellis wrote to Princess Alice: 'It is extremely difficult to keep conversation with Dame Helen consecutively on any one subject, or even to finish a subject; one cannot pin her down to definite statements.' To such a person, impregnable within the fortress of her own convictions, the very existence of the FANYs, with their tradition and panache, within *her* ATS, would present both a challenge and an affront.

Whatever the reason for that hostility, Dame Helen went to unseemly lengths to try and destroy the FANYs, even going so far as to delay the formation of the Motor Companies' Training Centre for four months, and then engineering the reduction of its intake by two-thirds – to the annoyance of Army Commands, who were desperate for drivers. Ironically, the Training Centre, when it finally started in February 1940, came under the Director of Military Training and South-Eastern Command, not DATS (Director, ATS). The Motor Companies, on the other hand, came directly under DATS.

For the first two years of their existence the Motor Companies, and from its inception the Training Centre, were very much the preserve of the FANY. As to the former, on August 1st, 1939 – a month before the outbreak of war – 1323 FANYs had been drafted into them, and in the next six months a further 549 were enrolled: as to the latter, during its first eighteen months, a total of 1259 FANY recruits went through the courses – initially lasting a month, later owing to the demand for drivers, reduced to a, more concentrated, fortnight – with a further 101 being sent direct to the MCs: a grand total of 3232. Until July 1941, the whole expense of the recruiting campaign for drivers on behalf of the ATS – 15,000 letters, a huge postage and telephone bill, all the stationery – was borne by the Corps, and the work done voluntarily by the staff at Headquarters.

In brief, the FANY contributed handsomely to the establishment of the transport side of the ATS during the first two years of the latter's existence, to be rewarded by the deliberate erosion of the members' allegiance to their own organization. 'These new members,' Kingston-Walker, Baxter Ellis's second-in-command (and later successor), wrote in the *Gazette* of October 1940, 'are just as full of FANY

*In her book *Service with the Army*, for example.

tradition as our old ones, and most keen to wear the FANY title on their arms. In fact, a large number of recruits were reduced, literally, to tears, when, at one period, certain members who wished to be FANYs but had enrolled through the ATS Recruiting Depots and not through FANY Headquarters, were forbidden to wear the flashes.' The wearing of the flash was eventually restricted to those who had been FANYs before September 1st, 1941. Despite which, the FANY continued to regard the Training Centre as their pigeon, and thus claimed the honour of teaching the Queen, then Princess Elizabeth, to drive in 1945.

No doubt there were faults on both sides, for it is quite obvious that the FANYs had little patience with – and even a certain distaste for – the new service. Kingston Walker wrote in the *Gazette* (August, 1942), 'Many auxiliaries from other units come with minds prejudiced against all ATS wearing the FANY flash . . . An elderly warrant officer . . . was asked how she was enjoying the course [at the ATS NCO's School]. "Oh, very much now, thank you ma'am, but I didn't think I was going to." When asked why not, she replied: "Well, you see, when I arrived I found I was sleeping in a barrack room with FANYs all round me, but do you know, ma'am, they are quite nice!"' On the other hand, ATS Staff Officers, Baxter Ellis reported to the Council, 'did not understand Transport work'; it seems that 'muddles occurred'; and there was, in addition, 'the unfortunate reputation of certain of the General Duties Companies'. This 'unfortunate reputation', exploited for all it was worth by the Beaverbrook Press, was to bedevil the ATS until well into 1942 when the Markham Committee finally scotched the rumours of moral and physical grubbiness.

This was an unhappy period for the Corps in general, and particularly for those members of it – far and away the majority – who found themselves involuntarily entangled with a brand-new service tersely described by Bidwell as 'a shambles'. To the FANYs' credit, however, let it be said that relatively few took advantage of the Adjutant-General's abrupt invitation, expressed at a stormy meeting with DATS and senior officers of the Motor Companies in April 1940, to those FANYs who were dissatisfied, to 'get out'. Nor, as was pessimistically forecast at one point, did whole companies resign en masse. Most, for patriotic reasons, stuck it; and, as the new Service settled down, accepted their lot with a good grace and the Corps' traditional energy and good humour. Nevertheless, many continued to subscribe to the Corps through the Regimental Association and Club: direct subscription to the FANY as such was forbidden.

The replacement of Dame Helen Gwynne-Vaughan in July 1941 by Jean Knox marked a rapid improvement in the management and morale of the ATS, and in its relations with the FANY. As able as her predecessor, and far less inflexible, she was only thirty, and as trim and svelte as Dame Helen was dowdy. Within a couple of years she and her deputy, Leslie Whateley, had turned the Service into an admired and indispensable part of the Army.

With these troublesome events behind us, we can now turn to what the FANY–ATS (known phonetically as Fannyats) were actually doing while the high-level wrangling was going on.

ii

The creation of the ATS was 'one of the most outstanding feats of military organization in the history of the British Army.'
Shelford Bidwell

'May I thank you ... for your pluck in carrying one (unexploded) bomb in the back of your car.'
Letter to FANY–ATS driver, July 8th, 1940

In April 1940 the first party of FANYs to cross the Channel for service in France since 1918 set off. Despite their ATS uniform, they were all members of the Corps, and were under the command of Senior Commandant Dr Joan Ince, one of the FANY's original two honorary medical officers. Their arrival coincided with the end of the 'phoney war'; and for a month they were employed on routine ambulance work. But on April 8th the Germans invaded Norway; and exactly one month later launched their *blitzkrieg* in the west, advancing, as Corelli Barnett describes it,* 'with a speed and ferocity that unnerved commanders still (despite Poland and Norway) expecting the deliberate unrolling of the 1914–18 offensive. Holland fell in five days. Meanwhile the roar of guns, the squeal of tank tracks and the terrify-

Britain and her Army.

ing scream of Stuka dive bombers moved on swiftly into Belgium and down towards France.'

The unit, which was in Dieppe, was heavily bombed, but suffered only one casualty, and was progressively withdrawn as the Wehrmacht raced westward to the Channel and 200,000 British and 139,000 French soldiers were crammed into the trap of Dunkirk, and, by June 3rd, miraculously evacuated. Thirteen days later the FANYs, who had finally succeeded in reaching St Malo through scenes reminiscent of the German offensive of 1918, followed them. Almost exactly four years were to pass before they set foot in France once more.

From a planned establishment of 17,000, the ATS grew steadily to a final figure of over 200,000; and by the beginning of 1942 the number of Motor Companies had risen from the original ten to thirty, with eleven more attached to AA Command. With the rationalization of Army Transport later in the same year, they were reformed into Command Mixed MT Companies, and so fully integrated into the Army. By such a mazy route, ironically, a large number of FANYs achieved what MacDougall in 1914, and Franklin in 1921, had attempted to do and failed. Indeed, Baxter Ellis became Senior Controller and Deputy Director ATS, and five Controllers and many Chief and Senior Commanders were FANYs, for once part of the larger service they were needed beyond the limited world of motor transport. Nevertheless, as Baxter Ellis herself had remarked in 1937, 'We are a transport service', and for the majority of FANY–ATS 'transport' or MT in its many guises was to remain their wartime job.

They might be in the RASC workshops, carrying out maintenance and repair work, or they might be ferrying 'Geraniums' about in Humber staff cars; driving real ambulances, or hurriedly adapted pantechnicons and delivery vans masquerading as ambulances. Sometimes the freight in the back might be something even more touchy than a dyspeptic colonel: an unexploded bomb, for instance, or an all-too-volatile crate of guncotton, primers and detonators.

iii

'I knocked over a man. He admitted it was his fault as he had been knocked over before.'
'To avoid collision, I ran into the other lorry.'
'A working gentleman offered to be a neutral witness in my favour.'
'I heard a horn blow and was struck in the back. A lady was evidently trying to pass me.'

Accident reports from Camberley, 1943-5

By 1943 there was virtually no department in the Army, apart from those in the battle-zone, without its contingent of ATS. Large numbers were attached to Anti-Aircraft Command (57,000) and the RASC (17,000), but they were to be found in countless other occupations: designing camouflage or making maps with the Sappers; virtually running the Army's blood-donor service; tracking the movement of shipping in coast defence plotting rooms or sorting letters in the Army Post Office; operating telephone switchboards and teleprinters with the Royal Corps of Signals, or reconditioning salvaged ammunition; running courses for ATS 'Other Ranks' with the Education Service, or helping to make training films. There was a small band of Military Police, and a select handful of rather high-powered personal assistants to Commanders and Chiefs of Staff. There were 24,000 involved in the training and administering of the other 183,000; and there were nearly 24,000 cooks. *Not* represented in this second war, however, was that splendid body of women of the first, the Women's Forage Corps.

All this was at home. From 1941 onwards the first contingents – apart from those briefly in France in 1940 – started to go overseas, and the demand for them, mainly as ambulance drivers and cipher clerks, quickly grew as the desert war ebbed and flowed.

The pattern of following hard on the heels of victorious armies held good in Europe after D-Day. The first small contingent of ATS landed in Normandy seven weeks later: two months after that there were over 6000, many – including Sheila Parkinson, then commanding the FANY-ATS SHAEF Mixed Command Car Company – with Supreme Headquarters in a variety of roles. Others went to East Africa where Farrar's FANYs – retitled the Women's Territorial Service (EA) – had been doing sterling work from the outbreak of war; and a handful to India, Ceylon and the Far East.

1921

9

The Free FANYS
1939–1946

'*The War Office has every desire to see the WTS (FANY)
continuing in existence but as a body separate from the ATS
and outside War Office control; it desires to help the
FANYs when possible and will gratefully accept its help so
far as the War machine permits. It was agreed that the
FANY might perform invaluable work as an entity with the
French, Finns or other foreign Armies as time goes on, or
under the Home Office.*'

From the Minutes of a meeting (February 7th, 1940)
between the Adjutant General and Sir Geoffrey
Lawrence, Chairman of the FANY Advisory Council

Baxter Ellis, already overworked herself, was determined that the
Corps in its pristine form – with which she had been closely bound for
twenty-five years and which she had nurtured and cherished as CO
for the past seven – should survive. The responsibility for sustaining
the FANY's tradition of versatile voluntary service wherever it was
needed was therefore handed over to those redoubtable sisters,
Marian and Hope Gamwell. In effect this meant virtually rebuilding
the Corps round a nucleus of old hands who, for one reason or
another, had not gone into the Motor Companies, and being ready
for, in the Adjutant General's somewhat patronizing words, 'invaluable work with foreign armies'. There was to be a pleasing irony
behind that dismissive attitude. Work with foreign armies there was,
and soon; but in due course a number of senior officers in the British
Army, too, would be finding the FANY doing 'invaluable work' in a
variety of fields and every theatre of the war. 'So many FANYs there

always seemed to be,' Irene Ward remarks from her own experience, 'it was always a source of conjecture how the supply could be so magically increased year by year.' They crop up all over the place.

The first call was not long in coming. In November 1939 Russia invaded Finland. For four months Field Marshal Mannerheim with 175,000 Finns 'outmanoeuvred and militarily humiliated' the one million Russians sent against them, only to be defeated in the end by sheer weight of numbers. By chance the wife of the Finnish Minister in London, Madame de Gripenberg, was an ex-FANY (née Moseley-Williams: 'Moses of the Belgian Convoy' no less) and when the Finns appealed for drivers for a unit of ten ambulances for their Red Cross, she turned naturally to her old Corps.

The forty volunteers were quickly found; Mary Runciman – known as 'Dicky' – was promoted from Ensign to Captain and put in charge; and an ex-member of Scott's last Antarctic expedition was co-opted to advise on the kit they would need, for the unit would be facing the northern winter. Owing to the military situation the expedition was postponed; but eventually, after a send-off by Princess Alice – herself soon to go to Canada where her husband, the Earl of Athlone, had been appointed Governor General – the convoy left Leith for Sweden on February 1st, 1940. By the time their vehicles arrived seven weeks later, to their intense disappointment the war was over: 'Every flag in Finland at half-mast ... towns congested with troops; men bitter and disillusioned, but steadfastly refusing to believe that such a Peace would have to be tolerated for long,' as Joan Lee wrote in the *Gazette*.

There was work to be done, all the same; and for the next few months the ambulances were busy picking up wounded and refugees – shades of Belgium, 1918 – and taking them to hospital or home. But by mid-summer the job was finished; by July they were back in England and the unit disbanded.

The enterprise was not a happy one from any point of view. Through no fault of theirs, the girls had been unable to do the job they had gone for; and within the unit there were accusations of insubordination, weak leadership, mishandling of funds, that rumbled on through the minutes of Advisory Council meetings for months. But then the spring and summer of 1940 had hardly been an auspicious period for expeditions. At least the Finnish convoy, however disappointing, demonstrated not merely that there was 'invaluable work' for the Voluntary FANYs, but that when the opportunity came they had the resources to take it.

ii

'*In June 1940, the French High Command agreed with the Germans that Polish forces would surrender along with the French. Sikorski refused, in a stormy meeting with General Weygand, and flew to London to promise Churchill that Poland would continue to fight. By the beginning of 1941, some 24,000 Poles had reached London and become the nucleus of a force which later grew to nearly 250,000.*'
      J. G. Beevor, SOE: Recollections and Reflections
                                                    1940–45

'*"Do you notice something?" I asked the girls a few days later.
"No," they said, "what do you mean?"
"The men are singing again!"*'
      Pat Beauchamp Washington, Eagles in Exile

The FANY's association with the Poles lasted from 1940 until the end of the war in Europe, and involved the kind of special relationship, an almost proprietorial feeling, that existed between the FANYs and the Belgians in 1914–18. After the German invasion of Poland on September 1st, 1939, followed by the Russian invasion a fortnight later, a great many Polish troops succeeded in escaping to the west, where they reformed into fighting units, 24,000 of them by sheer foot-slogging through Czechoslovakia, Hungary and Italy. They were concentrated in a camp at Coëtquidan in Brittany, and thither in the spring of 1940 Pat Washington (née Waddell) took a mobile canteen to supply them with some basic necessities, and a few luxuries. More than that, though, the girls – there were three of them – became a kind of surrogate family to these exiles. 'People came with all sorts of troubles, and sooner or later the inevitable pocket-case was produced with photos of wife and children, from whom as often as not they had had no news since the war . . . We represented home.'

On the fall of France Pat Washington and a great many of her protégés escaped to England, sadly without their canteen. The Poles were assembled in a series of tented camps on various estates in south-west Scotland, a variation on Coëtquidan, only bleaker. The lost canteen was replaced through private generosity, and with it Pat Washington and a number of other FANYs toured the camps until a rather more permanent *foyer* (a marquee) was established. Washington gives a romantic picture of the evening on which General Sikorski visited it. After the ceremonial, during which the General lit a symbolic fire of pine branches, the men sang first the traditional songs of their homeland and then, with less assurance, 'My Bonnie lies over the ocean . . .'

'The setting could hardly have been more picturesque, the hills around us were turning mauve in the evening light and long shadows fell across the beautiful park, while the flames rose high from the basket of pine logs, defiant like the spirit of the Poles. As a special surprise they sang "God Save the King" with perfect enunciation, and then with one accord they burst into "Yescze Polska nie zginela!" – "Poland will never die".'

From these modest beginnings, the Polish forces in Britain became one of the FANY's special concerns. Like the BEF, they had arrived with little more than the clothes they had on: to become once more a fighting force they needed uniforms, weapons, vehicles, equipment of every kind. Gradually they accumulated these things: what they had in abundance was fighting spirit and impulsive waywardness – and, as a kind of corollary, a formal courtesy. 'Poles can exasperate you more than any other race on earth,' exclaimed Pat Washington after waiting an hour for a belated lunch guest, 'and then they do something quite naive and charming, which utterly disarms you.' (The guest, a Polish captain, had been delayed through picking her some violets, which he presented with a formal bow.)

Two hospitals were allocated to the Polish forces, and the British American Ambulance Corps, with whom the FANY had close ties, provided ten ambulances, for which the Corps supplied the drivers. There were FANY staff-car drivers, a number of FANY-run canteens and, later on, a hostel in Edinburgh. Eventually a separate Scottish Headquarters was set up, first in Perth, later in Edinburgh, with Hope Gamwell in charge. The Polish military authorities' main fear was that the FANYs, being members of a voluntary organization, might be conscripted and spirited away, so they offered to put them on the pay roll. However, as they had no money and the bill would have to be met by the War Office, the proposal was turned down. They got their way in the end, and their FANY drivers were paid £5 a month. Many of the girls learnt Polish, some of them to such good effect that they were in demand as interpreters with the Polish ministries in London. They went on manoeuvres, and when units moved – when, for instance, the Poles took over part of the defence of the east coast of Scotland – the FANY canteens went too.

The FANYs who worked with the Polish forces – and there were at the peak about 250 of them – heard of the sufferings of that dark-starred, indomitable country at first hand: the living anguish of men whose parents, brothers, wives and children had been arrested, deported or murdered. Pat Washington describes how, at lunch in the mess, the Colonel asked her to translate a telegram which had been delivered to the table. The message was very short: 'Wanda and children sent to Siberia.' Wanda was his wife. From the wellsprings of their own compassionate humanity the girls had somehow to lend courage and strength to men so racked by uncertainty and grief. One senior Polish officer put it on record that he attributed the high morale of his men – proved in Normandy and again in Italy – at least in part to the warmth and sympathy which they received from the FANYs. At a rather humbler level, one anonymous 'Horse Artillery Man' expressed his feelings in the force's newspaper, *Polska Walczaca*:

'In canteens, hospitals, recreation rooms, headquarters and mainly as driving personnel, appeared these new ladies, unknown to us, becoming the first link between ourselves and the country which offered us hospitality at this critical moment. Their tact, kindness and courtesy, and their sincere desire to help, was for many of us in these difficult days of 1940 a bright ray in the midst of depression and sorrow.'

In July 1941, a month after the Germans had invaded Russia and only a year after the Russians themselves had occupied half Poland, a pact was signed between General Sikorski and Ivan Maisky, the Russian Ambassador in London, which restored diplomatic relations between them, and granted an amnesty to the estimated 1,750,000 Poles, civilian and military, who had been forcibly transported into Russia. This accommodation ceased abruptly two years later when the mass graves of Polish officers, slaughtered by the Russians, were discovered at Katyn. As always, Russian attitudes and actions were ambiguous and untrustworthy – as was to be demonstrated again in 1944 when they refrained from supporting the Polish Home Army during the disastrous Warsaw rising against the Germans – and ruthlessly dedicated to their own self-interest. During the interlude, however, a number of Polish women, as well as men, found their way to Britain; and the former were trained by the FANY and turned into units on the model of the ATS.

On June 5th, 1943, the aircraft that was bringing General Sikorski, his daughter, and his staff to England after a visit to Polish troops in the Middle East, crashed on take-off from North Front, Gibraltar, killing everyone on board. When the General's coffin was taken from Palace Gate where he had lain in state to Westminster Cathedral, FANYs from the Polish units joined the Polish ATS as part of the Guard of Honour, and were present, with members of Headquarters staff, at the funeral next day. Their presence, as the only British unit there, was a measure of the respect and affection in which they were held by the Polish forces.

The association was not limited to the United Kingdom. On Christmas Day 1943, a small party of FANYs who had been held up in North Africa on their way to Italy suddenly found themselves called upon to minister to a large party of Polish soldiers bound for the same destination. When they got to Italy, one of them wrote in the *Gazette*, 'one group . . . was put in charge of a convalescent depot in an old pink-washed farm house in the middle of olive groves, and the other . . . in a colony of little summer cottages high in the hills looking over the sea. Conditions were primitive . . . but we were supremely happy; and privately quite convinced that ours was the best FANY Section in Italy.'

'We were supremely happy': those four words with their echo of the spirit of Calais and St Omer, even of the camps of the inter-war years, epitomize the FANY style and go a long way towards explaining their popularity with those they served. In a regimented world they managed to combine the efficiency of the professional with the enthusiasm of the amateur, and that is a rare and precious thing.

iii

*'Abyssinia, Madagascar, the Red Sea Ports and SEAC
are their battle honours . . . the slouch hat and the wheel
badge have been seen in the War Office in London, in
Egypt, Syria and Palestine, in the Seychelles and in
India.'*
    Major Farrar, introducing the Service's History

The Section in Kenya was the only one formed outside the United
Kingdom. Started by Farrar with 16 members in 1931, its numbers
rose to 600 in 1941, with recruits from all over colonial Africa, from
Canada, Australia, New Zealand and Cyprus. In the notably
decadent white society of pre-war Kenya, the FANY Section was a
model of efficiency and enthusiasm. As if to anticipate criticism by
association, Farrar, in introducing the account of their wartime activities, wrote: 'An outsider reading through the book may think at
first glance that good parties and good food, pleasant quarters and
dances were the main interest of the unit, but . . .'. That 'but . . .',
since one good party is much like another, reveals a rather different
aspect.

Called up even before the outbreak of war, the Kenyan FANYs
occupied at first an even more anomalous position than those at
home, for they were a paid, African military offshoot of a voluntary,
unpaid English service. This was just the kind of conundrum to
fatten a War Office docket, and it took two years for a solution to
be found. In October 1941 the Kenya Women's Transport Service
(FANY) became officially recognized – retrospectively to September
1st, 1939 – as the Women's Territorial Service (East Africa) and a
military unit of the African Colonial Forces, under exactly the same
conditions of service as the men. However, despite the fact that, like
the FANY-ATS, their tie with the FANY at home was officially severed,
unlike them, they were still known as FANYs: they, of course, had not
been absorbed into a larger service, for in Africa no such service
existed.

Their first, and unpalatable, task was to act as guards to a large
group of 'enemy alien' women and children who had been rounded
up as soon as war was declared and interned in a camp, Mau Summit,
150 miles from Nairobi and at the bracing elevation of 8700 feet.

79

Guard duty was not one of the disciplines which they had practised at their pre-war annual camps, but they had five months of it before the 'prisoners' were repatriated: cold, tense, uncomfortable months, 'perched on the little treeless hill, with not another homestead to be seen for miles' and 'the icy wind whistling through the large cracks in the walls and through the door that would not shut...' But: 'It was fun, that Camp,' according to Corporal Wilma Blood; and certainly the girls were praised for their 'wise moderation and forbearance' in a pretty peculiar exercise.

For those not acting as warders there was plenty to do; ambulance and staff car driving, clerical and signal work, despatch riding, in and around Nairobi. 'The whole town seemed full of them,' wrote an ex-FANY who happened to be in the city. 'This may be partly due to the fact that they seemed to have the noisiest motor-cycles ever invented and when one couldn't actually see a FANY one could hear her.' And she goes on, '... the FANYs were employed because they were a responsible and disciplined Corps whose members could be trusted with secret and confidential matters. The whole of Nairobi had gone so secret one hardly dared to breathe lest the Italians in Abyssinia should hear it...'

And there, on Kenya's northern border, loomed the menace, and, in time, the opportunity. In October 1935 Benito Mussolini, dictator of Italy, had despatched a powerful force to invade and colonize Abyssinia in the face of the impotent indignation of 50 of the 54 members of the League of Nations. A year later the Rome–Berlin Axis was established, and thereafter, although Italy did not actually declare war until June 1940, she was an enemy power and a threat to British interests in East Africa and Allied traffic through the Red Sea.

In February 1941, amid all the other distractions of the time – Greece, Iraq, Syria – General Archibald Wavell, who five years later would become the FANY's Honorary Colonel, launched a three-pronged assault on the Italian forces in Abyssinia. Assisted by local partisans (trained by Orde Wingate) and a marked lack of spirit in the Duke of Aosta's considerable army, the campaign was all over in three months. Let Farrar herself, writing from Addis Ababa on July 27th, 1941, on official Italian Government notepaper tell the story:

'Six weeks ago ... General Cunningham ... agreed to let a small detail of the FANYs come up to work for the Occupied Enemy Territory Administration. They were desperately short-staffed as regards the senior officers and were completely lacking in clerical staff. The position was becoming chaotic, where a handful of men of the rank of Brigadier and Colonel were given the fantastic job of suddenly taking over the administration of a country of ten millions, plus the problem of a big intriguing Italian population, hating us on the one hand, but going in fear of their lives and having to be protected from the Abyssinians on the other, plus the constant threat of internecine strife... Six FANYs came up in the first batch, and even that tiny number made an almost incredible difference...'

After the six pioneers, more FANYs were summoned, not only to Addis Ababa but to half a dozen other spots: Asmara and Port Sudan on the Red Sea; Mogadishu in Somalia; and, after the invasion in May 1942, Madagascar. At Mombasa and Aden they worked with the Navy until the WRNS arrived, and in Nairobi itself and elsewhere with the RAF. Three died on active service, and eight more were killed in action at sea when their ship was torpedoed in February 1944. But even before that, as the war in the Far East swung to the offensive, a party of East African FANYs had been sent to Ceylon, the forerunners of many British FANYs who were transferred there from the Middle East and Italy during 1944 and 1945.

The Kenya Section was by no means the only link the FANY had with 'the lands of palm and pine'. Members of the Corps had always been great travellers – the *Gazette* between the wars is full of tales of intrepid journeys in out of the way places; they went abroad to work, or married men whose jobs were abroad. Conversely, a number of girls, mainly from the Dominions, joined when they were in England and remained members when they returned home. The Canadian connection was especially strong. There was a FANY Unit with the Canadian Red Cross, and the very fact that for the greater part of the war the Corps' President, Princess Alice, was in Ottawa as wife of the Governor-General, gave the relationship a special emphasis. There were similar, though less intimate ties with Australia, and in 1940 an organization with the portmanteau title of 'The Women's National Emergency Legion and Youth Movement' applied for and was granted affiliation.

iv

'The days and nights were the same, the nights with the wounded, the days with the dead. The last two ambulances went up in flames that night.'

FANY *Jean Dixon, after a raid on Devonport*

In the autumn of 1940 many of the male drivers of the Red Cross and St John Ambulance Companies were being called up, and, since they had no women drivers on their books, their Director of Personnel automatically turned to the Corps for help. There was, of course, a long history of co-operation between the two organizations; and so throughout the war some 200 FANYs drove Red Cross ambulances in Southern, Western and Northern Commands.

Drivers, FANY drivers in particular, in common with pilots of aircraft and small boat sailors, seem to develop an almost anthropomorphic affection for their machines. One remembers 'James', the motor-bath; and there were other, less eccentric vehicles which were given nicknames. Jean Dixon, quoted above, who drove through the blitz on Plymouth, wrote a perfect rhapsody to hers, 'an ambulance, an ordinary ambulance . . . but somehow older and far, far wiser' – and known, for reasons unexplained, by the unromantic name of 'Stanley'. Stanley and his chauffeur had many adventures, including having half a house land on top of him, but this was undoubtedly his finest hour. They had picked up a casualty and were heading for the hospital: '. . . the fires were terrific, whole streets blazing from end to end. Chased by bombs we fought our way towards the hospital. At last we reached the bridge, but too late – a bomb had fallen and half the bridge slipped into the river, the debris piled high. We could not turn back, so in bottom gear Stanley started to mount the bridge, his engine roared and the wheels spun: we held our breath as we wavered a few inches from the edge, then we were over . . . two ambulances died that night.' Good old Stanley! And good old Dixon, come to that!

That was just one incident among hundreds. Their stories, like those of the FANYS who drove for the American Ambulance Corps GB, are part of the saga created by everyone who was on duty in Britain's bombed cities and towns during that dangerous season: of threading through rubble-filled streets on dimmed headlights, past the glare of burning buildings, the whine and crash of bombs and the roar of the ack-ack guns; of the unseen threats of collapsing walls, falling shrapnel, flying splinters of red-hot metal or shattered glass; of the carrying of the wounded, the dying and the dead to over-worked, ill-lit hospitals; of the undulating whine of air-raid sirens and the whistles of air-raid wardens; of sleepless nights and haggard days, and the dark sky laced with the fingering searchlights as they picked out the tiny silhouette of a Heinkel or a Dornier, or glanced across the bulbous silver shape of a barrage balloon; of courage and kindliness and a controlled, cold fear in the pit of the stomach. Not for them the dubious sanctuary of an air-raid shelter or the squalid haven of a tube station platform. This was the Calais of 1917 writ large, demanding the same *'prudence et sangfroid'*. Fortunately *'le bon Dieu'* continued to *'protéger ses petites Fanies'*.

Bombs of the conventional kind continued to rain down, though with diminishing frequency and effect, for the next three years, to take their tithe of life and limb; then during 1944-45 came the uncon-ventional ones, Hitler's pets, the VI 'Flying Bomb' and the V2 rockets, unpleasant, dangerous and destructive, and once more pro-viding the ambulance and hospital services with unwelcome work. On June 6th, 1944, Allied forces returned to the European mainland over the beaches of Normandy, and, inevitably, the casualties started to flow back to Britain, many of them by air. Much of this sad traffic was handled by the FANY drivers with BRCS. Three months later, No 1 Motor Ambulance Convoy, consisting of 23 FANY and 23 Red Cross drivers, went rolling across the Channel in a Tank Landing Ship (LST) and disembarked on to the three-quarter-mile-long concrete jetty of the astonishing, prefabricated, floating Mulberry Harbour. 'We were a little dazed,' Alison Gatey wrote in the *Gazette,* 'and scarcely felt any surprise to be confronted with an orchard full of tents and a cookhouse and a water tank, and told that this was our location. It was all very peaceful.' (Only three weeks before, the German armour had been broken at the critical battle of Falaise, and the Allied armies, British, American and Canadian, were streaming across France.) 'It was during these first two or three weeks that we did more work than at any subsequent period . . . We met trains full of wounded which usually arrived during the night; we had a hospital carrier to load at Arromanches three or four mornings a week, leaving camp at 0530 hours. We also had air evacuations and hospital work.'

By Christmas – shades of the First War – and after a brief stay in Amiens, they were in Brussels.

Another girl, M. D. Lumsden, attached to the British Committee for the French Red Cross, found herself working for the French in a hospital from which, as they arrived, the German patients emerged with their hands up. 'A British General arrived, heard that there was one English girl working with the French Army, and asked someone to call me. I scrambled out of the lorry, very dirty and terribly hot, and went forward to him. All he said was, "What do you think you're doing here?" I answered that I was trying to help the French, and that I was a FANY. He laughed and said, "Goodness, you find FANYs everywhere and doing everything." I thought how very right he was.' Characteristically, she ends her report: 'I did not have one day free all the time I was out, and no bath for 3½ months. Still, I enjoyed it very much, and wouldn't have missed being a FANY with the French Maquis for anything.'

V

'The decrypts [were] sent down to Broadway from Bletchley by the car of a resolute lady in the FANYs, Mrs Barclay.'

Ronald Lewin, Ultra Goes to War

Churchill called the people at Station X at Bletchley who decoded German signal traffic 'the geese who laid the golden eggs but never cackled'. Although it does not seem that any FANYs were actually involved in that extraordinary academy, with its staff of international chess champions and poets, mathematicians and classical scholars, there is nothing odd about the fact that it was a FANY who, in the early days of the war, delivered the 'golden eggs' direct to the Prime Minister. For the Corps, having no general or particular brief, but having within its ranks many women of high calibre, acted as a kind of reserve of talent when there was work of special delicacy or high responsibility to be done. Thus they tended to turn up in high places: as drivers to very senior officers, or in a variety of posts in the War Cabinet, the Foreign Office, the War Office, and General Headquarters. In the hierarchies of war many FANYs occupied the rather exclusive, confidential position of the personal assistants and private secretaries of the hierarchies of peace: women with a unique insight into the web of power, and on whom their masters placed a total reliance. The FANYs involved in this type of work formed a separate HQ Attachments Unit.

The recruitment of these (and indeed all new members of the Corps) fell, with a thousand other tasks, to the small, overworked, and largely unpaid staff at Headquarters. In October 1940 they had moved house once again, this time to 31A Wilton Place, which was the Vicarage for St Paul's Church next door, and which the Vicar lent the Corps rent-free for the duration of the war. This was a gift from the gods, for 10 Lower Grosvenor Place was a strain not only on the Corps' precarious finances, but also on the staff's legs and tempers: being three floors up, they had to go trotting down to the basement every time there was an air raid.

With Mary Baxter Ellis totally involved with the Motor Companies and FANY–ATS problems, the Gamwell sisters (once referred to by a visiting soldier as 'the thin one and the thick one') took over the running of the Corps. Hope went north to command the Polish Units while Marian remained in London with an Adjutant (Elizabeth Hunt), an HQ Sergeant (Winifred Mason) and three clerks. In dear old William Cluff's place of Honorary Treasurer, they had J. A. Thomson, Managing Director of Brown's Brothers, and a director of Lucas. He not only succeeded in raising funds for the Corps among his friends in the motor trade, but, through Lucas, presented them with a very splendid mobile canteen for welfare work in the Far East.

The sheer amount of work that this tiny Headquarters team had to shoulder was quite daunting. Apart from recruiting, one of HQ's major labours – particularly as it included the Motor Companies ATS – there were training courses to be organized, records to be kept and updated, postings to be arranged, weekly reports from the units to be dealt with, the *Gazette* to be printed and distributed – twice a year until 1942, then once a year, but always subject to censorship. And all this against the sheer inconvenience of life in London in wartime: sparse public transport, little petrol, the disruption of bombing, and rationing. The last affected both the provision of uniforms, equipment – a local saddler with a stock of leather made all their belts – and trying to produce meals on demand for the FANY Club and Canteen. With no subsidies and no regular source of income apart from subscriptions, relying on gifts – and time and labour given without stint – the Corps always had a struggle to keep afloat financially. The balance sheet for December 31st, 1944, shows 'Cash at Bank and In Hand' amounting to £6810 8s 11d, and investments of £2830 7s 3d – not a munificent sum with which to run a Corps of 3-4000 members.*

In 1940 a number of FANYs were recruited as wireless operators for the Auxiliary Units (this was a clandestine army, formed by Colonel Colin Gubbins, which was trained to harass the Germans if they invaded Britain) and they also manned well-concealed radio stations during training exercises until they were finally stood down in 1944. One FANY who was involved remembers that contact was maintained through the local village post office in which the postmistress resembled nothing so much as Mrs Tiggywinkle, a homely comparison for such a potentially dangerous post. The secrecy was carried to extreme lengths: 'If you wanted a new toothbrush, a request had to be put in two envelopes!' Mercifully, the need for the Auxiliary Units never arose.

Once they had been established, Gubbins moved to an equally secret organization, and one in which the FANYs were to be involved on a considerable scale.

*Members who managed, nevertheless, to raise £2000 towards the cost of a Spitfire (total cost £5000), which duly had 'FANY' inscribed on the fuselage. Unfortunately there are no details of its operational record.

IO

The Secret FANYS
1940–1945
I · THE BACK ROOM GIRLS

'*To the organization they [the FANYs] were everything, as you well know, and without them we just couldn't have done it . . . They have been magnificent and invaluable.*'
General Sir Colin Gubbins to Marian Gamwell,
January 5th, 1946

'*And then there is Bingham's Unit, that bourne from which no FANY ever returns.*'
Ethel Boileau, *addressing newly-recruited FANYs at the training-school*

In the summer of 1940, Colin Gubbins, Director of Operations and Training in the newly created Special Operations Executive (SOE), was looking for two women to do confidential work. He knew of the FANY through Phyllis Bingham, Gamwell's secretary, because she was a family friend, and it was to the Corps that he turned. Gamwell, totally in the dark though she was, agreed; and Bingham and Peggy Minchin reported to 64 Baker Street, and were drawn into the mysterious, makeshift, murky world that went under the unrevealing title of Inter-Services Research Bureau.

However fortuitous or casual that initial contact, the result was a perfect match, for this was one of the occasions on which the FANYs' unofficial status was an asset: they could literally go anywhere and do anything without questions being asked; and SOE, for different reasons, was in the same case. It was not answerable to any of the

Service ministries, and the money it spent appeared in no identifiable estimate or account. The two services were, one might say, made for each other.

There is a measure of irony in the fact that what was undoubtedly the Corps' most dramatic contribution to the Second World War should have been in a field about which nothing was known at the time, and about which much that has emerged since has been concerned with its more lurid activities. The handful of women, many of them FANYS, who were trained as agents, dropped into Occupied France, carried out their lonely, nerve-racking work, and in a dozen instances suffered interrogation, unspeakable torture and brutal death, have, for their shining courage, inevitably received most attention. But they were only a very small proportion of the two thousand FANYS who served with SOE in Europe, the Mediterranean, and the Middle and Far East, in a variety of jobs which, while less sensational, were of equal importance in the evolving pattern of that fascinating organization. As Douglas Dodds-Parker justly observes:* 'Scores of books have been written about the many brave men and women who carried out the real work of resistance, in the field . . . Few have told of the minute application, the meticulous attention to detail, needed to put these . . . ideas into action.' And, with reference to the FANYS, 'They worked on every duty, from parachute packing to top-level staff duties' – and on the parachute that opened, the explosives that worked, the wireless messages that got through, the forged papers that passed scrutiny, as much as on the coolness of the agent, success depended.

ii

'We need absolute secrecy, a certain fanatical enthusiasm, willingness to work with people of different nationalities, complete political reliability.'
Dr Hugh Dalton to Lord Halifax, July 2nd, 1940

The origin of SOE is usually attributed to a Churchillian exhortation to Dalton after the fall of France, 'And now set Europe ablaze!' The combination of rhetoric and vision is characteristic; for, in a sense, this is what SOE achieved.

*In *Setting Europe Ablaze*.

SOE was formed in July 1940 from three existing secret intelligence organizations, with the purpose of stimulating by every possible means, legal or illegal, gentlemanly or otherwise, active resistance to the Nazi conquerors of Europe. Although some work had already been done on guerrilla warfare, notably by Major J. C. F. Holland and by Gubbins himself – who had brought some useful ideas back both from Ireland during the 'Troubles' and from Central Europe just before the war – there was no model for such a body in England. SOE had to be created virtually from scratch. As its existence as well as its purpose and operations had to be secret, the men who were brought in to create and run it tended to be known to one another and to come from the closed social circle of the better public schools. This reliance on a certain caste in the higher ranks – the actual agents were another matter – was undoubtedly one of the reasons why the FANY suited its purpose so well: they spoke the same language. In addition the girls, on the whole, were brighter than average, and their uniform, though obviously military, did not link them in any obvious way with any of the regular Services. In fact, FANYs turned up in so many different jobs that many people would have found it hard to say exactly what they did do, and this was an advantage in itself. It was particularly useful for the agents during their training: the FANY uniform gave them both a certain status and a form of protective colouring at a time when half the world was in one kind of uniform or another. (In the field, needless to say, it was different: neither belonging to the FANY nor anything else could save them from the loathsome attentions of the Gestapo if they were caught.)

SOE was divided into various Sections, each responsible for a separate country: thus F Section looked after operations in France; RF did the same, but in co-operation – theoretically – with De Gaulle and the Free French; and there were comparable sections dealing with resistance in Norway, Greece, the Balkans and so on. FANYs were closely involved with F Section, and most of the FANY agents operated in France; but a great many 'Special Unit' FANYs served with other branches, notably *Massingham* in North Africa, and Force 136 in the Far East. As for specific duties, undoubtedly their greatest contribution to the work of SOE in terms of importance, continuity and numbers employed, was in Communications, in both Signals and Cipher departments. Wireless, Gubbins said, was 'the most valuable link in the whole of our chain of operations. Without those links we would have been groping in the dark.' To which one may add the comment of M. R. D. Foot: 'This was the main operational work which the FANYs did, not only in Great Britain but all over the world.'

What was it like to be a wireless operator with SOE? Or on the cipher staff, coding and decoding signals? Those who were in it have the most vivid memories of those tense, often frustrating, occasionally exhilarating, always totally absorbing days.

iii

'The skill of the signallers and coders, and the courage of those in the field, tended to give the impression that it was little harder, and no slower, than sending a telegram at home.'
    Sir Douglas Dodds-Parker: *Setting Europe Ablaze*

'A more unruly lot I've never met!'
    Remark re FANYs attributed to Dodds-Parker

'Your daughter is now an unpaid driver.'
    Official letter to SOE FANY's parents

In 1941 Audrey Swithinbank,* eighteen-year-old daughter of a Suffolk parson, joined the FANY as a wireless operator, and in due course was called for a series of interviews at the offices of the Inter-Services Research Bureau in Baker Street. In that warren of cubicles she was intensively questioned, but told nothing. Neither then nor for many months afterwards would she have the faintest idea of the true nature of the job she was to do.

Accepted by SOE, she still had to undergo the three weeks of drill, lectures and chores at Overthorpe Hall near Banbury to which all FANY recruits were subjected. The course included one week doing all the filthiest jobs that could be found: 'I'm not quite sure why,' Audrey said, 'unless it was to instil into us the fact that FANYs had to be ready to do any job that turned up – in keeping with their unofficial motto, "I cope". They also impressed on us – "Once a FANY, always a FANY" – which I think is true.'

*Later Audrey Rothwell.

90

At last, suitably indoctrinated and fitted out with a uniform, she reported to Fawley Court, near Henley, for four months' intensive training in the Morse code. The required speed was 25 'words' per minute, which meant, since all messages were in code in five-letter groups, 125 letters a minute, or slightly more than two per second. 'While you're writing down one letter you're reading three letters ahead,' Audrey explained. 'Once your brain has mastered the technique completely, you never lose it.'

They had to sign the Official Secrets Act, and security was hammered into them as unremittingly as Morse: you were never, under any circumstances, to tell anyone what you were doing, nor discuss your work with anyone. Inevitably, since nothing in their relations with the regular services was ever perfectly simple, the FANYs in SOE carried a rank – Volunteer was the lowest – but were technically civilians, and unpaid at that. At the same time they were subject to Military Law. Abroad some of the girls held dual rank: non-commissioned Volunteers at work, Honorary Cadet Ensigns in the Mess, an arrangement well-calculated to discomfit members of more conventional services. Never was the designation 'good red herring' more applicable.

On completion of the W/T course, Audrey was posted to Grendon Underwood, a country house soon to be embellished with a hutted encampment (later an open prison) which was being used as a wireless station. It was at that point that her parents were informed that their daughter was now 'an unpaid driver', a message which, since to the best of their knowledge she did not know how to drive, only served to thicken the mystery of where she was or what she was doing. They never did discover until the war was over.

At Grendon Underwood the W/T operators were introduced to the Schedule or 'Sked', the observance of which was to dominate their working lives for the next three years. When they came on duty for their six-hour shift, into the long bare room with its benches and swivel chairs, its transmitter-receivers and Morse keys, under the minatory slogan REMEMBER THE ENEMY IS LISTENING, they would find on the noticeboard a list of the call-signs they were to listen out for, the time each was due, and the coded messages they were to send if and when contact was made.

The pattern behind these regular vigils was this. An agent, a 'Joe', who was sent into the field, had with him in easily destructible form his call-sign, his code – usually the 'one-time pad'* – and his copy of the schedule. But there were many reasons why a strict observance of the 'sked' might be impossible, and weeks or even months might elapse between an agent going into the field and his first making contact. Sometimes they might never be heard from at all; but until confirmation of their fate filtered through, the listening watch had to be maintained. The excitement when, after an interminable silence, an agent at last came through, was intense, but tension was in the very air they breathed. Audrey has not forgotten the occasion when the Morse she was receiving turned into a continuous buzz, and was then abruptly broken off. She waited in vain for the transmission to be resumed, and only learnt much later that the operator had been surprised at his set by the Gestapo. They had shot him through the head, and he had fallen forward on to the Morse key.

Immediately the text of a message had been received it went to the decoders. Many messages would be accurate and intelligible: equally, many would not. Poor atmospheric conditions, jamming by the enemy, or simply mistakes made by an operator working under stress, could all result in signals that only time and patience and infinite ingenuity could unravel. To the cipher staff – known balefully as 'cipherines' – such conundrums were an added fascination to a job which all of them found absorbing, and most found obsessive. Paddy Sproule, who was in both North Africa and Italy, remembered that when there was a corrupt signal to be elucidated, no one would think of going off duty until the problem was solved. They became like crossword puzzle addicts and Mil Walker† always talked of coding as the love of her life.

By no means all Special Unit FANYs were involved in signals. From 1942 onwards SOE expanded at an accelerating pace, the number of agents to be trained increased, and more and more Special Training Schools (STSs) were opened. Some of these specialized in wireless operation, for FANYs or for agents or for both; others covered the various skills which the 'Joes' were required to master. At most, if not at all, of these schools there were FANYs. There were FANY drivers and despatch riders, clerks and accountants, cooks and orderlies, W/T operators and instructors, and coders.

*For details of the various code systems, see *SOE in France*.
†Later Mrs Lobanov-Rostovsky.

These were the girls who vanished into 'Bingham's Unit'; for Phyllis Bingham was responsible for recruiting them and, in the widest sense, looking after their health and welfare. Increasingly, also, from 1943 onwards, she was expected to supply wireless and coding staff to serve abroad, and those who were posted to SOE Headquarters in London. These girls were involved in every kind of work from making maps to keeping the signal register, from briefing agents to broadcasting those cryptic messages over the BBC's overseas service which informed Tante Louise that her niece's cat had been run over – a message that might mean, to the initiated, that a forthcoming supply drop had been cancelled.

At the end of 1942 the Eighth Army had won the decisive battle of El Alamein; on November 8th a powerful Anglo-American force had landed in Algiers, and although the campaign became bogged down during the winter, on May 13th, 1943, the last Axis forces in North Africa surrendered. The first members of SOE landed with the invasion. Sir Douglas Dodds-Parker arrived a day or two later, and set about creating Inter-Service Signals Unit 6 (ISSU6), codenamed *Massingham*. 'Our radio station,' he writes in *Setting Europe Ablaze,* 'was soon working into Corsica and France, as well as keeping essential links with Britain and Tunis. Most of the work of signals and coding was carried out by the FANY. A party of ten had come out in November 1942 in the ship *Scythia* which had been torpedoed but had limped into Algiers. Others arrived in 1943 until a total of some 250 were serving in the theatre. Their uniforms and badges were unusual, so they were all, rightly, treated as officers. All spoke at least one foreign language.'

Audrey Swithinbank was one of them. Because she was under twenty-one she had to have her parents' permission to be posted abroad, and they hesitated for a long time before granting it. She arrived, with twenty-two other FANYs, at Algiers in the *Orion* in May, and was based at what had been a rather select seaside resort for wealthy Algerians, the Club des Pins. 'Our billets,' one of the girls wrote in the *Gazette,* 'were villas perched high on the sand-dunes. They were almost completely bare of furniture, but we soon rectified that by improvising packing-cases . . . which we garnished with paint.' 'The heat and glare were tremendous,' wrote another, 'not to mention the smells!'

At the Club des Pins British, Americans and French – including agents – lived and trained within the same encampment; and for the first time the FANYs actually met the men and women with whom they would be in radio contact. They were a mixed lot; from an ex-Legionnaire, ex-safe-breaker, Audrey was to learn the art of picking locks – though she does not reveal if this particular skill has ever come in useful.

The Allied arrival in North Africa, then in Sicily and, in September 1943, their first landings on the Italian mainland enormously increased the scope of SOE's operations. There were agents and partisan groups not merely in Corsica, France and Italy itself but throughout the Balkans, most notably in Yugoslavia; and with more aircraft available and shorter distances to be flown, SOE and its American sister service, OSS (Office of Strategic Services) were able to pour in agents, arms, explosives and equipment. The resulting signals traffic was prodigious and ever-growing, and kept the signals staff flat out.

Between the first landing at Reggio and the second at Salerno, south of Naples, Italy, with Mussolini deposed and Marshal Badoglio in charge, made overtures through intermediaries in Lisbon to break with her Axis partner and surrender. The negotiations which led up to this went under the rather unkind codename of 'Monkey', and the word was to become extremely familiar to the signals staff at the Club des Pins. Douglas Dodds-Parker gives something of the exuberant flavour of that heady time. The preliminaries concluded, the Italian emissaries arrived in North Africa to conclude the negotiations. Dodds-Parker had their rooms bugged. 'Their conversations were listened to by the Fannies [sic] who translated them and sent in the typescripts with jugs of coffee.' 'Ungentlemanly, no doubt,' he adds disarmingly, 'but surely justifiable!'

But the terms still had to be agreed by Badoglio in Rome. Speed was vital, for the Salerno invasion force was on its way. Communications were handled by SOE staff through a British agent who was actually in Rome. Would Badoglio accept the terms?

'So we waited,' Dodds-Parker records. 'Then about six one evening Mary MacIntyre, the FANY coder, came in with a look of excitement and a rather scruffy piece of paper. On it was a message in Italian, accepting the Armistice terms . . . Contrary to standing orders and discipline, I kissed Mary.'

It was this feeling of being at the centre of events, of actually knowing the agents who were working their sets in the mountains of the Haute Savoie or in the Apennines far behind the German lines or at Tito's headquarters, that gave the job its fascination. Another FANY, Peg Tod, wrote: 'Even though more and more people were involved, the work, although better organized, grew and grew. Coders no longer worked shifts but worked until they could work no longer. W/T Operators practically slept at their sets.' And she describes their feeling 'of such tremendous fascination in the work that it was virtually impossible to keep away; and then, inevitably, the most terrible tiredness.' To which Audrey added, 'But we didn't care. We would volunteer for coding and decoding when we were off duty we were so completely involved in it.'

With a spirit like that, one need hardly be surprised that the FANYs were popular with those for whom they worked. But that is not to say that they did not enjoy life as well; in fact, for a crowd of energetic, lively-minded young women, life at the Club des Pins was a full one: extremely hard, interesting work, interspersed with plenty of excitement and fun. There were endless dances – it was a point of honour, not always too graciously observed, to attend those for other ranks and not just the officers' – and strictly illegal escapades such as hitch-hiking trips in service aircraft. From the normally inevitable consequence of being found out, being sent smartly home, the three wireless operators who were flown to Corsica on one of these jaunts, and then couldn't find anyone to fly them back, were only saved by the timely invasion of the South of France. Their skills were so badly needed that necessity overrode retribution.*

Altogether there were about 250 FANYs in *Massingham,* and their OC, Staff Commander Hume Henderson, reported that it 'became one of the happiest FANY units overseas . . . Everyone could see what they were doing. They could watch field personnel being trained, doing their jumps on the sand-dunes, and they had contact with agents by coming to know them before they went into the field.' During demonstrations laid on for visiting top brass, it was not unusual for one of the FANYs to make a parachute jump with the agents. Such participation was a far cry from those early, blinkered days at Grendon Underwood.

*Audrey later married the pilot – Group Captain Rothwell – who flew them there.

'Our Mess consisted of two white marble houses with imposing pillars, verandahs and balconies. Lights blazed from every window – there was no black-out in Cairo.'

Mercer, *Gazette, 1945*

'Conditions were primitive . . . In the farm the only water had to be drawn from a well, and our only lights were hurricane lanterns.'

McLachlan, *ibid.*

As the war in the Mediterranean moved up the slow length of Italy, the FANYs moved with it, first to Monopoli and Torre a Mare on the Adriatic coast, halfway between Bari and Brindisi, and later to Siena. The country was suffering from the normal dislocations and deprivations of war: 'There was very little running water,' one FANY wrote, 'and the electricity was spasmodic. Italian servants proved to be the most notorious thieves.' The winter was bitter, and they were driven to sneaking coal out of the engine-tenders.

They coped, of course, both with such minor domestic problems and with a mounting work-load. The nature of the work was changing, from the clandestine to the more overtly military; the secret armies of Europe, the resistance groups, partisans, maquisards, began to coalesce and take more and more audacious action. To help them do so, nearly a hundred three-man teams known as *Jedburghs* were dropped into France in mid-1944, and all of them had to be included in the communications network.

Reports in the Corps files for these years, 1943–45, give a clear picture of how stretched the organization was. Not only were more and more trained wireless operators and cipher staff being demanded and having to be found, but there was a shortage, at times quite desperate, of officers and NCOs to look after the essential administrative machinery.

There had been FANYs – living, by the sound of it, the life of Riley – in Cairo since 1943, among them a number of Kenya ATS (EA) and local civilians. Marian Gamwell, whose wartime travels form a saga on their own, and who had originally gone to Egypt to set up the necessary organization, herself gave them their FANY induction course. War or no war, the uniform was not to be used to give a paramilitary respectability to every Sue, Meg and Maria who needed it. Many of these members of the Corps, old and new, were transferred to Italy.

As one European country after another was wrested from the enemy, so FANYs in small parties, even in ones and twos, found themselves being swept off to Athens, Toulouse, Paris, Brussels and Germany itself, to help with the inevitable aftermath of war. And with victory in the West assured, and the armies in the East moving forward against Japan, they were desperately needed there, and volunteers were called for. The story of Force 136 is dealt with later: it is time now to enter that crepuscular world known as 'the field' into which the 'Joes', men and women, were despatched during the years 1942–44, many of them never to return.

1936

II

The Secret FANYs
1940–1945
II · IN THE FIELD

*'I am very often asked why we liked women for under-
ground work in France . . . Women were suited to the job
as they could move about more freely in occupied territory . . . Eventually, of course, several women couriers
were called upon to fill a man's place after a sudden arrest,
and woman wireless operators did the same work as the
men.'*

Miss Vera Atkins

In early 1942, following a Cabinet decision, the first women to join
SOE as agents were selected and sent for training. By 1944 just over 50
had been sent into France, 39 of them FANYs, or WAAFs who became
FANYs on recruitment to SOE. Of those 39, 13 were murdered by the
Nazis. Of the rest, some were captured and tortured, but survived;
others stayed free by the skin of their teeth and performed prodigies
of valour.

The stories of many of them have been written, though rarely by
them themselves, and made into films, and are now part of the myth-
ology of the Second World War: here we have space only for certain
highlights to illustrate something of what was entailed, and illumi-
nate the courage which they displayed in circumstances well-
calculated to break the bravest of mortals.

Since a perfect or near-perfect knowledge of French was almost
the first requirement for an agent, inevitably the majority of women
agents were either wholly or partly French, or had lived in France.

Thus Andrée Borrel, who was a courier in and around Paris – she was variously described as 'the untameable', 'the best of us all', and *'un garçon manqué'* – was French; Yolande Beekman was born in Paris of Swiss parents; Madeleine Damerment was the daughter of the Head Postmaster of Lille, and spent two years on the Allied escape lines in Occupied France before escaping to England and joining SOE; the incredible, indomitable, Russian-born Indian princess, Noor Inayat Khan, had lived in France; Vera Leigh, forty years old and 'the best shot in the party', was, in all but parentage, a Parisienne with her own couturier business; Eliane Plewman had an English father and a Spanish mother and had lived largely in France; and Diana Rowden, for all her English looks and education, had spent much of her youth along the shores of the Mediterranean, where her parents had a yacht, and was in France at the surrender. Total familiarity with France and the French way of life was even more important than a perfect accent; and few if any agents were caught because of their speech – though it behoved some of them to be careful. Nothing, not the most perfect protective colouring, nor all the training in the world, was proof against the handful of skilled and plausible traitors who sometimes succeeded in infiltrating a circuit.

ii

'I doubt – therefore I survive, must be the motto of every successful agent.'
> M. R. D. Foot, *SOE in France*

'If it had not been for the stately homes of England, I do not see how we could possibly have got on with the war.'
> John Goldsmith, *Accidental Agent*

Of the 73 FANYs who were trained as agents, only 39 actually went into the field. The ones who completed the intensive four-month course may be compared to the astronauts of a later date: they became members of an élite as arcane as the priesthood of Apollo, acolytes of a mystery close to the heart of life and death.

Training, if scrupulously observed in the field, could do much to keep an agent out of German hands – and to help him retain his integrity if he were caught – and the training imposed on its 'students' –

men and women alike – by SOE was directed to those ends. Essentially it consisted of a number of batches of separate skills. In the first batch, conducted at Arisaig on the west coast of Scotland, were hard physical training, 'silent killing', fieldcraft, weapon-handling, sabotage, and a whole battery of similarly essential, if anti-social skills. At Ringway aerodrome – the second stage – they did their parachute jumps; and at Beaulieu in the New Forest they learnt the essential arts of espionage: the inviolable laws of security; the constant vigilance; how to spot and shake off a follower; how to make contact with other agents; the routine of the 'safe house', the cut-out and so forth. The climax of the general training was an exercise lasting several days, in which each agent had to find his way cross-country alone to an address in a strange town, and, having been caught, undergo an unpleasantly realistic interrogation by SOE staff in SS uniforms. It was not a course of training for the delicate, the hot-headed or the faint-hearted.

Throughout, the FANYs were accompanied by a conducting officer – a FANY, naturally – whose task, to quote from the files, was to act 'as a liaison between the recruits under her charge and the various Training Officers. She takes part in all the training with the recruits with a view to sharing their life and obtaining an insight into their characters and reactions . . . their motives for joining . . . their fears and hopes. The recruits are trained with and by men, and are usually in a very small minority . . . The conducting officer has to see that her charges observe all the security regulations . . . She makes periodic reports to HQ as to how the recruits are shaping.'

Those who were to become wireless operators attended special courses in using the sets – large, heavy and difficult to conceal as they were – and in cipher work. Yvonne Baseden, Yolande Beekman, Inayat Khan and Diana Rowden were all sent to France as W/Ops: they and the men who trained with them were the senders of those coded messages which Audrey and her colleagues listened for so intently; and when the call-signs and the security checks came through, the messages passed back and forth, the circle was complete. Another 'Joe' was established in the field.

But between the end of training, the adoption of a new name and occupation, the final, meticulous preparation, and actually landing in France might be, particularly in the winter, a long and harrowing time. It was spent at special holding schools where, according to Knut Haukelid,* 'A number of service women kept the house in order, cooked the meals, and gave the boys some social life. They belonged to the special section called "Fannies" [sic] . . . They were always willing to come to Cambridge in the evening for a little party . . . But if we asked the Fannies about our comrades who had gone out before us, they became dumb and knew nothing.'

At last a date and a time for departure were set – though they might easily be postponed. This was the moment for that final, minute checking of everything from the labels on clothes to the most insignificant of personal possessions that might betray where the agent had come from; and, conversely, the provision of all the oddments, the identity cards, ration books, old bus tickets, snapshots – created, forged, or brought back by returning agents – that built up and confirmed the fictitious persona which the agent was to assume. Then, the drive through the night to Tempsford or Tangmere, the Lysander or Hudson waiting on the tarmac, the last-minute checks, the brief goodbyes and good lucks, the dwindling engine-note as the aircraft took off and headed east for the dark and dangerous world beyond the Channel. And the silence.

⋮⋮⋮
iii

'She had lodgings quite near me, for months I would watch her tripping along the pavement in the morning, so busy, so affairée. She was of no interest to me; so long as she kept out of my way, she could play at spies.'
Hugo Bleicher, Abwehr Sergeant (quoted by Elizabeth Nicholas, Death Be Not Proud)

If Bleicher was speaking the truth – and he was the most notorious and one of the most successful members of the German counter-espionage service, the Abwehr – those two sentences epitomize the chilling game of cat and mouse that was being enacted in the cities and country lanes of France during those years. Vera Leigh had been flown into France by Lysander in May 1943 as courier in one of the circuits operating in and around Paris. Several of these had already

*In *Skis Against the Atom*.

been penetrated by the Germans: five months after her arrival she was arrested and interrogated. Nine months later, with Andrée Borrel, Diana Rowden and Sonia Olschanesky, she was murdered and cremated in the concentration camp at Natzweiler in Alsace.

Paris and its environs were no place for an agent in the latter half of 1943. Andrée Borrel, after a dashing and highly successful year – she had been the first woman agent to parachute in, in September 1942 – as courier to François Suttill, was arrested there; so was Noor Inayat Khan. A particular radiance of tragic courage illumines this strange Indian girl, 'a splendid vague dreamy creature', as one fellow agent described her, 'far too conspicuous ... and she had *no* sense of security', a girl who had once written children's stories for Radio Paris, finding herself at the centre of a fairy-tale far more fearsome than any she could ever have imagined. The circuit, *Prosper*, to which she was attached and its satellites were being methodically liquidated round her; day by day the agents she was supposed to work with were disappearing, until she was the only SOE wireless operator still operative in the whole of Paris. She survived in this shadowy, disintegrating world for four months, even succeeding in making contact with London, reporting the names of the agents who were still free, and arranging an arms drop. But the Gestapo were already on her trail – their detector vans had picked up her transmissions – and she was arrested in October. Under interrogation she disclosed nothing; twice she tried to escape; she refused to give parole, and was sent to Dachau, where, eventually, they murdered her in September 1944.

The ripples from the *Prosper* débâcle swept outwards to engulf Diana Rowden, trapped by an impersonator in her sawmill hideout at Clairvaux near the Swiss border in November 1943; and Madeleine Damerment, 'the brave, young and gentle' girl from Lille, who, with two companions, was faced with that worst of agents' terrors, to be met on landing in France by a reception committee, not of members of the local Resistance but of members of the Gestapo from their headquarters in the Avenue Foch. With Noor Inayat Khan, Yolande Beekman and Eliane Plewman, she was murdered in Dachau.

Not all were taken so easily. Violette Szabo, a lorry driver's daughter and described as 'one of the best shots and the fieriest characters in SOE', on her second foray, ran into a German ambush and shot it out with them until she ran out of ammunition. With two other women agents, Denise Bloch and Lilian Rolfe, she was murdered at Ravensbrück in February 1945. And Yvonne Rudellat, the first FANY and one of the first of SOE's women agents to enter France, also made a fight of it. She was landed on the Riviera coast in August 1942, and established herself in the city of Tours, close to the border between the Occupied Zone and Vichy. Here, in addition to working as a courier, she organized reception committees for incoming agents and supplies, and is credited with blowing up a couple of locomotives. She was shot trying to escape from a German control post – after a gun-battle, according to one version – was wounded and captured. After a period in Ravensbrück, she was transferred to Belsen, at which place of horror by an almost unbearable irony, she died, unknown and unnoticed, soon after the camp was freed by the British.

Vera Leigh, identified, watched, tailed, pounced upon when the time was ripe: Yvonne Rudellat and her companions blundering by ill chance into an unexpected checkpoint: two extreme examples of the perils that lay like a minefield round the daily life of an agent. None of these women was caught through her own mistakes or shortcomings; their misfortune was to be attached to circuits which, unknown to London, were already compromised. Often, however, it was simply a matter of time and luck. Odette Sansom was arrested after seven months, to survive both torture and Ravensbrück, a story of fortitude which through much telling first made the world aware of the work of the women agents. Of the two Nearne sisters, Jacqueline remained at liberty, the pretty containers which she carried as a traveller in cosmetics packed with explosives or radio spares for her circuit in central France, until she was safely flown back to England; while Eileen, a FANY wireless operator, who followed her and sent back a mass of useful information from Paris, was arrested at her set in July 1944, survived Ravensbrück, and finally escaped from a camp in Silesia.

From the accounts of their precarious days, the oppressiveness of life in a country occupied by an enemy as thorough and as ruthless as the Germans continually comes through; and with it, the appalling strains clandestine work imposed on those courageous enough to undertake it. It is dangerously easy, however, to overemphasize the dark side: many thrived on the risks, and were inspired by the knowledge that the work they were doing was of value to the Allied cause. And one remembers Lise de Baissac, the Mauritian girl who built up a circuit bicycling round the countryside south of the Loire under the pretence of collecting geological specimens; and later, with her brother Claude, both training the maquis in weapon-handling and, after D-Day, gathering information on German dispositions and passing it on to the Allies. So steady was her nerve that she actually rented a room in a house occupied by the commander of the local German forces; so buoyant her spirit that when the last Germans had gone and the Americans arrived, she was wearing her FANY uniform which she had kept hidden but ready for this triumphant moment.

Lise worked for a time with Mary Herbert – who later married Claude de Baissac – a FANY, and the first WAAF to volunteer for SOE, with the circuit known as *Scientist,* and, like her, survived unscathed. Yvonne Baseden, though she too survived, was not so lucky. For the months before and after the Allied invasion of Normandy she was in constant radio contact with London, as well as turning out for drops of arms and supplies; but then she and seven of her colleagues were trapped in their cheese-factory headquarters during a routine search. Although they all managed to hide, they were winkled out, one by one, and dragged off for interrogation. After torture, and a suicide attempt which she was too weak to execute, Yvonne was sent to Ravensbrück. 98,000 women died – were murdered – in Ravensbrück: Yvonne was one of the ones whom the Swedish Red Cross Unit found alive when they reached the camp in April 1945. But she was in hospital for six months as a result of the brutality and privation.

From among all the names, each one synonymous with gaiety and courage and an indomitable spirit, from the separate hells of the interrogation rooms and the basement dungeons, the concentration camps and the gas ovens, it is refreshing to turn to two women gifted with such ebullience and fire and good fortune as Nancy Wake and Pearl Witherington. The first, blessed with Australian high spirits and Australian toughness, moved from the Pat line – the most famous and successful of the escape routes, organized by Albert Guérisse, alias Lieutenant-Commander Patrick O'Leary, RN – to a circuit called *Freelance,* bordering the west bank of the Rhône, which eventually mustered a trained maquis force of 5000, for whose prowess she was largely responsible. The second, Pearl Witherington, also took to resistance work as to the manner born. With her fiancé, Henri Cornioley, she assumed the task of cutting the main line from Paris to Bordeaux with such efficacy that the Germans put a price of one million francs on her head. No one ever claimed it: indeed, in June 1944, when the carefully nurtured secret armies of France were at last given free rein, her circuit, *Wrestler* (with its neighbour, *Shipwright*), was responsible for 800 separate interdictions of the railways of Indre et Loire; and German reinforcements struggling north to join the battles in Normandy took a very long time over the journey indeed. In this, and in a thousand other instances, the work of SOE and its dedicated members of all nationalities, both in the field and out of it, achieved its ultimate justification.

Immediately after the war in Europe was over, the Intelligence Officer of F Section, SOE, Miss Vera Atkins, to whom that section's agents were in the nature of a family, took upon herself the task of trying to discover exactly what had happened to those who had been sent to concentration camps and had disappeared without trace. With little official backing, indeed often in the face of official indifference, she got herself attached to the legal staff conducting the Nuremberg War Trials as a Squadron Officer, WAAF, and, almost singlehanded, set out to trace survivors, camp commandants and guards who knew of their fate, and extract from them sworn statements. At the end of what she herself describes as the most harrowing year of her life, the task was done. This is one example of such a statement, made to her by Obersturmführer Johann Schwarzhuber of the SS, camp overseer at Ravensbriick.

'I declare that I remember that I had delivered to me towards the end of January 1945 an order from the German Secret Police countersigned by the Camp Commandant Suhren instructing me to ascertain the location of the following persons: Lilian Rolfe, Danielle Williams [alias Denise Bloch, a FANY] and Violette Szabo. These were at that time in the dependant camp of Königsberg on the Oder and were recalled by me. (All of them were in a pitiful state and Lilian too weak to walk.)* When they returned to the camp they were placed in the punishment block and moved from there into the block of cells.

'One evening they were called out and taken to the courtyard by the crematorium. Camp Commandant Suhren made these arrangements. He read out the order for their shooting in the presence of ... (various camp officials, including the doctor) . . . I was myself present. The

*From Vera Atkins's covering letter to the War Office.

shooting was done only by Schult with a small calibre gun through the back of the neck. They were brought forward singly by Cpl Schenk. Death was certified by Dr Trommer. The corpses were removed singly by internees who were employed in the crematorium and burnt. The clothes were burnt with the bodies . . .

'All three were very brave and I was deeply moved. Suhren ("the miserable Suhren", V.A.) was also impressed by the bearing of these women. *He was annoyed that the Gestapo did not themselves carry out these shootings . . .'*

Sgd: Johann Schwarzhuber.

*Author's italics.   1939

I2

FANYs Far and Wide
1943–1946

'*The next big moment in their FANY career is embar-
kation, which has its effect on the Hostel ... There is an
atmosphere electric with excitement, mingled with a wist-
fulness that is very near to tears – two years is such a long
time to be away from home!*'
M. E. Foster, Captain i/c FANY Hostel, St John's Wood
Park, September 1945

'*After all, I am her mother and I must know!*'
Ibid.

It was 1943, the year in which the tide of war began to turn decisively
in favour of the Allies. The Germans were out of North Africa.
British, American, Canadian and Polish troops were back on the
mainland of Europe, if only in Italy. The Russians had stemmed and
were now beginning to roll back the German assault from the Baltic
to the Black Sea. In the Pacific the US Navy was in the process of
taking its revenge for the disaster of Pearl Harbor; and in Burma, at
the end of that year and in the first months of 1944, the Japanese were
accorded their first defeat – at Imphal and Kohima – and, for the first
time since their original advances in 1941, were in retreat.

The formation of South-East Asia Command (SEAC) under Lord
Louis Mountbatten and the build-up of the Fourteenth Army under
General Slim were accompanied by the expansion of SOE's Force 136.
SOE had been operating in the Far East in a limited way from the start,
sending 'parties of specially trained men into occupied South-East
Asia,' to quote one writer on the subject, 'in order to supply the guer-

rillas with arms and collect information. They were operating in Johore from 1944 onwards, and they were either dropped by parachute or landed by submarine. Among them was a number of Chinese agents whose job was to gather intelligence, and who were in radio contact with their HQ in India.'*

Extension of such operations meant a growing demand for secretarial and cipher staff and W/T operators – and that meant the FANY, particularly in forward areas, where it was felt only women in uniform should serve. And so in January 1944 the first five FANY officers went out as confidential secretaries to Supreme Allied Commander South-East Asia (SACSEA). In addition, a number of civilian women who had already been recruited into Force 136 were inducted into the FANY.

In spite of the end of fighting in North Africa and the rundown of *Massingham*, the Italian campaign was still grinding on, and D-Day was in the offing. Those members of the Corps who were serving in the Mediterranean theatre were, many of them, overdue for home leave; and by no means all were prepared to volunteer for a further spell overseas. For this reason, a great many of the six hundred or so FANYs who went out to the Far East from September 1944 onwards – Margaret Foster noted that 753 had been through the St John's Wood Hostel in those twelve months, not all of them bound for SEAC – were young (between eighteen and twenty-three) and not fully trained. That same report describes them on arrival as 'frightened little people not knowing quite what to expect, but very eager to learn and to look like the other FANYs they meet floating around the houses'. (After the statutory two weeks at Chicheley Hall, she notes, they return 'fully-feathered FANYs, ready for training and bursting with the Corps spirit and history'!)

Their destinations were widely separated. Meerut, forty miles from Delhi, saw the first FANY Indian section, followed by Colombo, Poona, Calcutta, Kandy, Trincomalee and Rangoon, with detachments in half a dozen other places. The oddest, and most sought after, was undoubtedly Kunming in China, the railhead that linked the Burma Road to Chiang Kai-Shek's headquarters at Chunking. Altogether eight FANYs made that exciting flight 'over the Hump', and into a world even stranger than the tea plantations of Ceylon or the bazaars of Calcutta.

A Fearful Freedom, Robert Hamond.

If the work was familiar, living conditions 'out East' were not, and their letters and reports are vibrant with the novelty of living in palm leaf huts, the attention of personal servants, the sounds of the jungle at night, the soporific wafting of the *punkahs* operated by the big toe of the *punkah wallah* squatting in a corner of the Mess. Of one amenity, if that is the word, there was no shortage – men. The FANYs were in constant demand; and as Jill Merriman, FANY Staff Commander OC Indian group, reported wryly, 'It was more a case of limiting late passes to prevent members' work suffering, than of searching for entertainment.' And in one respect the FANYs, young and inexperienced though they might be, showed that the traditions of the Corps were in good hands. Merriman goes on: 'Although military personnel were supposed to take leave in the command in which they worked, FANYs became incorrigible in "hitching" air lifts to the more far-flung parts of the theatre, in the face of much official opposition' – 'official' meaning, presumably, Merriman herself!

There is no doubt, however, that the Indian Group presented the most tortuous administrative problems, not only at home, where the hard-pressed staff at Wilton Place had to recruit, train, kit out, brief and despatch successive batches of girls into the blue – and the vagaries of wartime transport were a tribulation on their own – but on the spot. Most of the drafts landed in Bombay; and in the twelve months between September 1944 and September 1945, a total of five hundred FANYs arrived, thirty at a time, every three weeks. New to the tropics, inadequately kitted – Merriman has some caustic remarks about the quality and suitability of the ATS uniforms with which they were issued, and the myth of the solar topee – they had to be held in hurriedly prepared transit camps for ten days or so to become acclimatized before being packed off to their stations.

By May 1945 the Fourteenth Army had recaptured Mandalay and Rangoon and were pressing on towards Thailand and Malaya; and in July a detachment of FANYs was in Rangoon. Then, on August 6th and 9th, atomic bombs were dropped on Hiroshima and Nagasaki. Five days later the Japanese agreed to unconditional surrender, and the Second World War was over.

The end of hostilities meant the disbandment of Force 136 and thus, in theory at least, the end of the FANYs' work. In practice, with a mass of administrative and other problems pressing, Allied Land Forces

South-East Asia (ALFSEA) saw a chance to acquire a hundred or more efficient, well-trained girls for signals and clerical work. But – not for the first time – the Corps' curious 'red herring' status worked against it, and the War Office vetoed the transfer.

The girls were furious. Their overseas contract had been for two years; many of them had more than a year to run, and, like Conrad, the East had them in thrall. While the War Office was mulling it over, however, a number of girls were loaned here and there: about a dozen to the higher Command for cipher work, seven to Saigon, two to Kuala Lumpur as secretaries, and one as personal assistant to the Duchess of Gloucester – the Duke was Governor-General of Australia. Another FANY was personal assistant to Lady Mountbatten. A few, who could find civilian jobs, were demobbed out there, as were those who had got married and whose husbands were serving in the theatre; but for the majority it was the transit camp at Poona, now working in reverse, and the long wait for ship or aircraft to take them home. To keep them busy and out of mischief some instructors were rustled up, and the girls were subjected to lectures on such improving subjects as dressmaking, driving, and dramatic art. But not until the spring of 1946 was it possible to close the Poona section finally. What had begun as a great adventure had declined into something very like a fiasco.

ii

'May I, as an ex-PoW recently arrived in Madras from Singapore, take this opportunity to express my deepest appreciation of the wonderful work which the members of your organization are carrying out on our behalf . . .'
H. E. Witheford, Captain IEME

The Fourteenth Army, slogging through the jungles of Burma, had come to regard itself, with some justification, as 'forgotten'. About the only welfare they ever saw in their war, described by one historian as 'bitter, hazardous and awful', was that provided by the all too few stalwart ladies of the Women's Auxiliary Service (Burma), with their few static and mobile canteens. Early in 1945 the Army Council, aware of the deficiency, invited the FANY and the WVS to send out units to supplement this meagre provision.

There were not many unemployed FANYs, nor, indeed, many unemployed women at all, in Britain at that time: however, volunteers were combed from the Polish Welfare Unit and Corps members who were working with the Red Cross; and the Burma Unit – otherwise known as the FANY Welfare Unit SEAC or the FANY ALFSEA Unit – duly set out for the Far East.

Whatever role they expected to fill in the Far Eastern Theatre – and welfare, as one of them wrote, 'is a particularly elastic word as applied to the FANYs in SEAC' – they, like their colleagues who had served with Force 136, were at the mercy of events. The Japanese surrender in August revised all preconceptions. Without a scintilla of doubt, though, the most necessary, nerve-racking and valuable job they undertook was to welcome back to freedom the thousands of living skeletons released from the prisoner-of-war camps in Burma and elsewhere. These sick and starving men needed food and clothing and medical attention; above all, perhaps, they needed the warmth of human kindness after years of disease, brutality and constant, circumambient death; and this the FANYs were proud and pleased to give.

By October 1945 the last prisoners of war were on their way home, and the girls were able to turn to other aspects of welfare; taking round mobile libraries, for instance, and running canteens, attending innumerable dances (not always the delight the word might suggest!) and organizing – that old FANY speciality – various forms of entertainment. The Army of Occupation was now scattered all over South-East Asia, and FANYs found themselves carrying out these heterogeneous duties in Saigon, in Bangkok, in Tokyo, in Borneo, and even on the island of Morotai in the Moluccas. From such a variety of places, and an equal variety of occupations, one can only pick out one or two particularly piquant details. In Bangkok they ran an institution for British other ranks which was known as The Oasis Canteen; while in Japan the club at Tokishima rejoiced in the name of *Ichi Raku Ya* which, being interpreted, means apparently 'The House of Great Pleasure'.

In Singapore, among more routine chores, the following account from the *Gazette* suggests devotion beyond the call of duty spiced with a strong element of comedy:

'O'Hagan and Miles went to the Docks late at night to find the firemen trying to put out a blazing Chinese junk. The junk was towed out into the bay, and the FANYs followed in a launch with the tea urns, biscuits, cups, etc. While transferring to a barge, the tide started to turn and the barge was swept away with Miles and the urns only aboard. After much searching in the dark they found each other again, and finally served out welcome tea and eats ... Our average number of cups of tea served has been 5000 per day. The "scrounging" of wood to keep our water boiling could only have been done by FANYs who, somehow, manage to get things where nobody else can.'

On Labuan Island, North Borneo, the girls lived, at some risk of being brained, under canvas in a coconut grove, and earned the following compliment: 'How nice it is to have the FANYs and the WVS as they will talk to the boys, whereas the other women about tend to ignore anyone without a pip on his shoulder. Who said the FANYs were snobs?' Who, indeed? A similar, if rather racier, testimonial was offered to two of the girls when it was known that they were due to leave Malaya:

'You know, miss, the people that selected you FANYs knew their job. One day the Mobile Canteen arrived with two real ladies. They talk nice and are very good for us – the next day they send two comics like yourselves! But you all do a good job of Welfare for us chaps, and I expect we'll miss you. Shame you're going so soon.'

Quite the best story of all from these strange days in the aftermath of war comes from a Canadian girl, Lieutenant Joan Bamford-Fletcher. She was in charge of a section detailed to get returned PoWs out of Sumatra, that huge, jungly island, a thousand miles long, which is separated from Malaya by the Straits of Malacca. By the middle of October there was only one lot unaccounted for, 2000 women and children stuck in a camp 500 miles from Padang, the nearest port; and only one person left to rescue them – herself. The internal political situation was volatile; the Japanese, though no longer belligerents, were still there; and the few British troops were restricted to their own areas.

'I arranged with the Japanese Army Headquarters,' she wrote in the *Gazette*, 'for a convoy of fifteen vehicles: this was increased at various times to as many as twenty-five.' The trip involved a climb to 5000 feet through the mountains, and a ferry crossing which took on average two hours and was usually done in the dark. 'I made that crossing twenty times in thirty days,' she wrote. 'The roads were narrow and very rough . . . We started the convoys with forty armed Japanese as guards, and finished with seventy and machine guns mounted on the trucks. I worked with nothing but Japanese and was the only British person on the convoys. It shook the Japanese a bit to find themselves under the command of a woman. On the third convoy in Padang I got caught between a 15cwt and the jeep and got dragged down and my head cut open. The blood was terrific, but I went to the hospital and had three stitches put in, and two hours later we were on the road . . . From there on, the Japanese couldn't do enough for me. My interpreter told me they had discussed it that night, and he said he would like me to know, I had won the respect of every man on the convoy, but they had decided they would never marry a European woman, they were too tough. Anyway after that I never passed a Japanese on the road without being saluted . . .

'Towards the end of the convoys the Indonesian situation became rather tricky, so I put a crash car at the head of the column with a big wide bumper to crash the barricades they put on the roads . . . We had one bit of trouble though, on the second last convoy.' One of the private cars, driven by two Dutchmen, which was accompanying the convoy, had been commandeered by Indonesians, and the Dutchmen had disappeared. Bamford-Fletcher arrived just in time. 'I pulled the jeep up alongside and opened the door and just said "out" and out he got! I then put the five armed guards on the cars and went off with my interpreter to find the two Dutchmen. We found them in a small house with all their personal effects on the table in front of them, with an Indonesian waving a great bloody knife in their faces, another with a revolver and the head man questioning them. My interpreter said they were British and must be released immediately. He swore and yelled about the Empire and what not to add a little colour and eventually we got them out through a milling crowd of about 500 who had gathered at the noise. I must say I was rather glad to get out of that hole . . .'

She concludes the account as follows: 'The Captain of the Motor Coy came out to Pakan Baroe on the last convoy, and thanked me for my courteous treatment of his men and presented me with his sword, "in token," he said, "of his respect and esteem". I felt very gratified.

It is a 300-year-old one and very nice.'*

The war was over. From outposts all over the globe, and from nearer home, from Germany and Norway, from Czechoslovakia ('Never before have I realized what a precious heritage it is to possess British citizenship,' Captain J. R. Aldis wrote to the *Gazette* from Pilsen, as she watched the pathetic streams of refugees streaming in from the Russian zone), from Greece and Italy, and from all corners of the UK itself, the units came winging home to be demobilized and take up the new/old life, and, a great many of them, to get married. ·(One enterprising FANY, Daphne Green, even managed to get married on Labuan Island.)

Simultaneously the ATS were also being demobbed, and many of the FANY–ATS chose to return to their old allegiance. Among them was Baxter Ellis, who for a brief period resumed her position as CO, thus allowing Marian Gamwell and her sister to return to their neglected farm in East Africa. We shall catch glimpses of this remarkable pair from time to time during the coming years; but in 1946, as they prepared to go back to their beloved Africa, the senior members of the Corps had no doubts as to their contribution – Marian's in particular – to the FANY's record during six years of war or the Corps' status at the end of it. Baxter Ellis may have been responsible for the survival of their independence as the Free FANYs: it was Marian Gamwell who, to a large extent, was able to put that independence to good use. The Regimental Board, meeting on June 4th, put on record their appreciation of her 'strength of character, superb moral courage, clarity of vision, determination, business acumen and powers of endurance'. When it is remembered that at its peak during the Second World War, the Corps had a strength of 6000, 2000 of whom were with SOE – a delicate operation which Marian Gamwell masterminded throughout – and that her wartime travels took her to Algiers and Cairo, to Italy, and, a historic trip on its own, to India via Persia which she reached by hitching a lift across the desert in a truck, the encomium does not seem extravagant. And this was, as it remains, a voluntary organization, whose existence had been only grudgingly recognized by the military hierarchy.

That the Corps had achieved so much was largely due to Marian Gamwell: that it had been capable of meeting the successive chal-

*The sword went to Canada: she was made an MBE.

lenges which she supplied was due to a tiny nucleus of administrative officers, operating under every sort of difficulty from common shortages to flying bombs at headquarters, at the hostels and training schools, and at the various units. The Regimental Board mentioned four in particular: Hope Gamwell, as Second-in-Command; Elizabeth Hunt and Winifred Mason at 46 Wilton Place; and L. M. Freeth at the FANY Training Centre.

There were other marks of approval. During 1945 Gamwell had been summoned to Buckingham Palace with four members of SOE to describe the work of the Special Unit to the Queen; and to Marlborough House to do the same for Queen Mary. And in October of the same year, Princess Alice, on leave from Canada, paid a visit to Headquarters, her first since she and the Earl of Athlone had left for Ottawa in 1941.

The final expression of the 'wartime spirit', the final explosion of euphoria, came with the Victory Parade of June 8th, 1946, in which thirty FANYs from all ranks, Units and theatres of war took part with representatives of all the forces, including those from the 'Dominions and Colonies', which had fought in the war. They had five days' training; and then, 'as the great day dawned' – to quote Elizabeth Hunt, who wrote a fulsome description of it for the *Gazette* – they were all taken in army transport to the starting-point in Hyde Park: 'It was rather like diving into the sea, thousands and thousands of faces, the overwhelming roar of the cheers, one's breath was taken away by the tumultuous welcome, flags waving, the good-humoured crowd who had sat up all night for this moment to greet the representatives of the services of the Empire, who were marching to see their King.'

Yes, the Corps had put in a good and useful war, and had come out of it with their reputation for efficiency, versatility, and a certain joie de vivre enhanced. They deserved their moment of glory. But, as before, over the future hung the Damoclean question-mark: what role was there to be for the good old 'red herrings' in the cut-price, cut-throat, nuclear world ahead?

13

The End of Euphoria
1946–1965

'That is a very bald statement of a very great achievement
by a Corps of Women who did their duty as they saw it.'
                                                    Princess Alice

'FANYs will have to begin to think ... about the future of
the old Corps. It has got to live ... [but] it is impossible to
envisage at this stage what the future may bring.'
                                                            Ibid.

On October 26th, 1946, HRH Princess Alice, Countess of Athlone,
the FANYs' Commandant-in-Chief since 1933, officially opened the
Corps' Regimental Club at 55 & 56 Sloane Street, London, SW3. This
seemed at the time an event of great importance for both the present
and the future of the FANY. There were between eight and nine
thousand serving or recently demobbed members – over 3000 of
them FANY–ATS who were welcome to rejoin the Corps and/or the
Club if they wished; the spirit of wartime was still burning brightly;
and the Club, with its pleasant lounge, dining-room and bar,
provided exactly the right atmosphere to keep that flame alight.
Indeed, for the nineteen years the lease of the two properties had to
run it proved a popular meeting-place, as well as a convenient headquarters; but by the late 1960s the inevitable dispersal of members,
their absorption into other ways of life, and the gradual fading of
wartime memories and wartime comradeship, except among the
most determinedly nostalgic, were eroding its support. Even if the
lease could have been extended, or other suitable premises found, it is

doubtful if it could have been kept going for many more years. Within a year or so of its opening, even, the cry was going up for more members; and its finances were always precarious. Nevertheless, for some years after the war ended it was very popular.

In her speech at the opening, Princess Alice gave a 'very bald statement' of the Corps' wartime doings which have been the subject of the last few chapters. The achievement is perhaps all the more striking when the numbers involved and the range of work accomplished are compared with those of the previous war: *Massingham* and Force 136, the Motor Companies of the ATS and the Polish Unit, SOE and the Far Eastern Welfare Units, Singapore and Sumatra, Bangkok and Labuan, were an aeon away from Lamarck and Camp du Ruchard, St Omer or the Calais Convoy.

Whether the 'continuous training' which HRH divined as having been the secret of past success, as well as the prerequisite for future usefulness, could be maintained in the narrower, less clear-cut context of post-war Britain was uncertain. 'Wars,' as the newly appointed Honorary Colonel, Field Marshal Wavell remarked, 'are quite the most expensive form of national living, and have to be paid for' – which meant, as usual, economies in the Services. And there was a new threat to the Corps now: during 1947 the War Office finally decided that the ATS should be re-created on a permanent basis as the Women's Royal Army Corps; so, for the first time in peace, the FANY had to compete with a properly established, official women's corps. The immediate and discouraging result was that, at the end of 1947, the Army Council informed the CO that they were 'unable to allot a role for the WTS (FANY) in the Post War Army'. The consequences of that rejection, after two decades of official, if sometimes half-hearted, recognition, form the underlying theme of the Corps' history for the next twenty-five years.

That year saw other changes, too. Mary Baxter Ellis and Tony Kingston-Walker had returned to the FANY from the ATS in 1945 as Commanding Officer and Second-in-Command respectively, but their regime was short. They retired together in 1947 and, inseparable as ever, went off into the country to breed cocker spaniels and paint in water-colours. They were to die within a couple of months of each other twenty years later. Baxter Ellis had been a FANY for over thirty years and CO – apart from her time in the ATS, of which she became Deputy Director – for fifteen. Building on Lilian Franklin's secure foundations, she had prepared the Corps for its wartime expansion, and, by fighting off the various attempts to destroy it – and by summoning Marian Gamwell to run the independent Corps Units – had ensured that the Free FANYs would survive and prosper. With her faithful Ganymede she left a notable stamp on the character of the Corps.

Baxter Ellis's successor was Maud MacLellan, a Scot, who had been a FANY since 1929 and had gone to the ATS, in which she had risen to command the MT Training Centre at Camberley before returning to the Corps when the war was over. She was as devoted to the FANY as any of her predecessors, and brought to it great warmth and imagination; but she was beset, particularly during the latter years of her command, by ill health and family problems, exacerbated by the geographical drawback of living in Scotland. In any case she could hardly have taken over at a trickier time; for as she wrote in the *Gazette* in March 1948: 'Our former peacetime activities have been of great use in the past, but most of them will now be undertaken by the permanent Women's Services.' Transport, for example, was no longer worth pursuing. MacLellan saw that their best hope lay in cultivating a number of specialist skills which the regular services tended to ignore. The FANY, she said, must 'strike out on new lines', and she adumbrated 'Radio-Telecommunications, knowledge of foreign countries and their language, secretarial and staff duties, mechanics and welfare work'. Twenty-six years after that appreciation, the first two items on her list still figure largely in the Corps curriculum.

In order for such specialized subjects to be worth the effort of learning, and to provide the Corps with a secure basis, they needed sponsors, the seal of approval of some department of officialdom which would commit itself to saying, as the War Office had done after the General Strike, that in an emergency it would be calling upon them to do certain specific jobs. But the late 1940s were a time of financial stringency and uncertain adaptation to the realities of a nuclear world; organizations like the FANY, however meritorious their war record, did not find it easy to convince the powers-that-be of their value.

Rather more of that record gradually began to seep out of the files during those years. In 1950 the BBC Home Service broadcast a series entitled 'Now It Can Be Told', one of which, 'I Cope', gave a vivid picture of the FANY agents with SOE and their training. Jerrard Tickell had already published *Odette*, his account of Odette Sansom's adventures and privations in France, and in that same year the book was filmed, with Anna Neagle in the lead. A party of FANYs, who appeared in the early sequences, were invited to the set at Beaulieu, where both Odette herself and her surrogate quickly captivated the members of the Corps. Anna Neagle was made an honorary FANY – Mrs Sansom (then Mrs Peter Churchill) was one already, of course – and subsequently attended many of the Corps' annual reunions, including that of 1983.

A less transient tribute than books and films and radio programmes to the fifty-one FANYs – agents and others – who died on active service during the war, was a Memorial Tablet, placed on the outside north wall of St Paul's Church, Wilton Place: that pleasant, quiet corner, just out of the surge of Knightsbridge traffic, which had been the heart and brain of Corps organization for most of the war and to which every FANY must have come at one time or another. It was unveiled on May 7th, 1948, by the faithful and indefatigable Princess Alice; a brief service has been held there each Remembrance Sunday since.*

In the meantime the proposed structure of the post-war Corps was being created. Country groups were being formed in Lancashire, Worcestershire, Yorkshire, Northumberland, Scotland, the Home Counties and Dorset, with others to come in Essex, Hertfordshire and Hampshire. Training along the lines laid down by MacLellan was organized; and in 1950 the first post-war camp was held. The site was frankly a bit of a comedown: a transport café at Teddington Hands, near Tewkesbury. Forty members attended, lived under canvas, and continued MT training, with one important difference: for the first time they had the use of a device known as the 'Handy Talkie', an early form of walkie-talkie, and a pointer to future interests.

Throughout these years, familiar names are scored through by death. Sir Evan Gibb (Honorary Colonel 1933–1946) in 1949; Lord Wavell in 1950; Lady Ernestine Hunt (at the age of eighty-one) and

---

*Among the little group of mourners who attended it in 1983 was one of the sisters of Yolande Beekman. She placed a potted cyclamen among the wreaths and bronze chrysanthemums with the message: '. . . *à ses chères soeurs*, Dora, Sonia and Diana.' Such is fidelity.

Dr Joan Ince, one of the FANY's first two medical officers, in 1953; Lilian Franklin in 1955; and in the same year, L. M. Freeth, MBE, who had been at St Omer, and had run the Training School, Chicheley Hall, during the Second World War. And, anticipating a little, Grace MacDougall died at the age of seventy-six in 1963, and Lady Hailsham two years after her. With the deaths of Franklin and Mac especially, almost the last links with the mad, brave days of Captain Baker and his dizzy daughter were snapped for good, those days the inception of which, as Princess Alice remarked in a happy phrase in the Corps' Fiftieth Anniversary Year, 'had been so haphazard, so bold and impractical'.

ii

'*Competitions for the Company Cup included a drill competition won by A Company, tent-pitching won by B Company, and a night exercise including map reading, a treasure hunt, an RT exercise, a driving test ... and cocoa and sandwiches round the camp fire.*'
Gazette: Camp Report, 1953

1953 was Coronation Year. The FANYs, ever patriotic, were not well-pleased to be told that they had 'no official part to play in the celebration'; though they were at least represented, by the CO, who was allotted a seat in Westminster Abbey, and by the four girls who were given seats in the Mall. However, thanks to the Foreign Office connection, twenty-five FANY drivers were on call for a visit by the Commonwealth Parliamentary Association, and had to conduct their charges through the throngs which crowded London for the occasion. It was better than nothing.

Perhaps with the idea of counteracting a certain sense of being officially unwanted, and, more positively, to put the Corps' achievements on record, at about this time Baxter Ellis asked her old friend Irene Ward, MP for Tynemouth and a valiant champion of the FANY – though never a member of it – to write its history. The outcome, *FANY Invicta*, appeared in 1955, and was happily described as being 'not only factually complete and accurate ... but also succeeds brilliantly in giving the atmosphere of the old Corps which is so essential'. Considering that Dame Irene (as she was to become and subsequently Baroness Ward) was primarily neither a writer nor a historian but an extremely busy woman in public life, *FANY Invicta* – despite its rather forbidding title – was a brave and conscientious attempt at telling the FANY story. It has long been out of print, and has become, inevitably, out of date as well, hence the present account.

An invaluable source for any such work is the *Gazette* which, replacing Mac's short-lived *Women and War*, has appeared continuously, the war years included, since 1910, and records the fortunes of the Corps and its members with spirit and humour.* Much of the material in the immediate post-war years was contributed by ex-FANYs who were working or had settled abroad, particularly in Africa. Two tiny items are worth a mention: in the autumn of 1956, and sporadically for a year or two thereafter, there appeared a page devoted to the mysteries of make-up. Like recipes, this may have been a sign of editorial desperation; but one remembers that in *Massingham*, Douglas Dodds-Parker put out an edict forbidding the wearing of jewellery on duty, and one girl who refused to conform was actually sent home. The veto did not, however, extend to lipstick. The second item was the first mention of classes in unarmed combat, which soon became 'the most popular item on the programme' – as, under its current military title of CQB (close-quarters battle), it still is. Another extramural activity, which is still on the agenda and still well-attended, was rifle-shooting, for which, in that jubilee year, Princess Alice presented a challenge cup in the form of a rose-bowl. It was duly noted that the first woman to win the King's Cup at Bisley, Marjorie Foster, was a FANY.

iii

'The FANY Corps has the oldest traditions and the proudest record of all women's corps in this country, and therefore the greatest spirit.'

Field Marshal Earl Wavell

The Corps' Fiftieth Anniversary caused, as might be expected, a rush

---

*Pertinent extracts from those of the Second World War, selected by Jane Brown, were printed privately in 1983 under the title of *As We Saw It*.

of memories to the head. Eight FANYs, among them Tony Colston, veteran of pre-1914 days, representing the 'Seven Ages' of the Corps, had an audience of HM The Queen; MacLellan was awarded the OBE; and at the Aldershot Show nearly sixty FANYs presented a pageant in four episodes to illustrate those fifty years of history. There was a ride in period uniforms; a stirring mock-battle of the kind envisaged by Captain Baker; a parade of vehicles from both wars; and a reconstruction of the work of SOE, complete with an agent being dropped by parachute to a reception committee of the Resistance. All these, rounded off with a special Jubilee Reunion held in Chelsea Royal Hospital and attended by more than 300 FANYs, combined to make 1957 a memorable year.

The Corps had come a long way since those days when, as Mac recalled in the *Gazette*, 'We drilled on the roof of Gamage's Buildings in Holborn, and were openly laughed at and jeered at as we went to and fro.' With a history of the Corps in print, a sense of Royal favour, a newly minted motto, *Arduis Invicta* ('In Hardships Unconquered' – or, in FANY langauge, 'I Cope') and a formal, if tenuous, arrangement with the Communications Department of the Foreign Office, they had good reason to feel proud of themselves and their traditions, and rather more confident about their future.

And the reminiscences kept on flowing: memories of St Omer and the ammunition dump that blew up, and the other similar disaster at Andrich; memories of Lamarck, and of 'Lewis playing Handel's *Largo* on the cello while I fried the sausages for our midnight supper; of doctors with long black beards, and of everything being incredibly insanitary and uncomfortable.' Happy days! And, from the more recent war, Maurice Buckmaster describing how the presence of women had a steadying effect on the men who commanded them, while 'their resourcefulness more than once saved the lives of their less fortunate colleagues'. From all these stirring tales the memory of the Corps' past was kept evergreen: surely they must point to a future of equal flair and opportunity?

The distinction of the Corps's Honorary Colonels over the years reinforced this conviction. Field Marshal Earl Wavell was succeeded in 1952 by Major-General J. A. Gascoigne, CB, DSO, General Officer Commanding London District. He served until 1959, when Lieutenant-General Sir William Scott, KCMG, CM, CBE, took over. Major-General Sir John Anderson, KBE, replaced him in 1971; to be succeeded in his turn by the present holder, Major-General C. E. Page, CB, MBE, BSC (Eng), FIEE, former Colonel Commandant of the Royal Corps of Signals. Although they do not figure largely in this narrative, their position in Army hierarchy and their practical advice and help have proved invaluable over the years. Several of them had seen the FANYs' work during the wars, knew their worth, and were ready to support them in their determination to survive in a largely indifferent world. Similarly, the Chairman of the Advisory Council from 1933 to 1965, Lord Oaksey – formerly Sir Geoffrey Lawrence, and a highly distinguished lawyer – was the FANYs' staunchest friend and supporter, particularly during the difficult period of the formation of the ATS. He, as much as anyone, ensured the continuation of the Corps as an independent, voluntary organization.

iv

'The Spirit of friendliness and humour [of the Kenya FANYs] ... set standards for me which will, with your help, give me the insight, tenacity and ingenuity that I shall need to help us find fresh fields in which to serve.'
Sheila Parkinson, on taking over as CO, Spring 1965

Maud MacLellan, wholehearted as she was in her devotion to the FANY and its interests, was beset by family problems and was not herself in good health. She was finally forced to resign, relinquishing command in February 1965, after seventeen difficult years.

Her successor was Sheila Parkinson – the present Commanding Officer. Her selection of the qualities which she recognized in the FANY, and those which she deemed necessary for the job – quoted above – was shrewd and revealing, for, combined with great warmth, humour and independence of mind, they are her own.

Starting as a Kenya FANY in 1937, Sheila Parkinson had returned to England on the outbreak of war and joined the FANY–ATS, serving first with one of the MT Companies, then with a Mixed Transport Company of the RASC in the West Midlands, and finally as CO of the FANY–ATS Mixed Force (SHAEF) Car Company. In this last capacity it was her lot, soon after D-Day, to get sixty FANYs, four taxi-drivers, and a mixed bag of rather grand Daimler staff cars and Generals' caravans from Bushey Park to Versailles. It was an epic journey – involving strike-bound docks, a drunken ship's captain, and heavy seas that not only caused seasickness but also put the taxis in some danger of sliding off the deck – but eventually they arrived at Versailles and lined up their vehicles on the gravel in front. Their reception was much what they might have expected: after a time, a red-tabbed staff officer strolled out and looked at them fishily. 'Oh, there you are,' he said. 'You're late.'

'We'd been eleven days in our clothes, we were not a pretty sight, and we were famished,' Sheila Parkinson rounded off this saga. 'But as one looked at our strange fleet of vehicles ranged before that magnificent facade, one couldn't help feeling a certain sense of achievement. And that's what it's all about.' Although technically carried out under the aegis of the ATS, it was a fairly characteristic FANY enterprise, both in its execution and in its outcome – and somebody, no doubt, said they loved every minute of it.

After the war Sheila Parkinson spent fifteen years as Personnel and Welfare Officer with the Kuwait Oil Company, travelling frequently to the Gulf on their behalf, and all over the Middle East by cargo boat and tramp steamer on her own: her idea of a holiday is still the precise opposite of the packaged variety. As valuable as this zest for life, in her new job, was the fact that her time in SHAEF had given her considerable experience of the workings of the Army, and a lot of friends on whom, twenty years later, she was quite prepared to exercise her 'insight, tenacity and ingenuity' on the FANY's behalf. Her assumption of command in February 1965 closes one chapter in the post-war annals of the Corps, and begins a new and more hopeful one.

14

Small, Compact, Efficient
1965–1984

'I joined the WTS (FANY) to do something completely different and something useful. How different it would be I had no way of telling, but up to now, I've not been disappointed.'

Di Hammett in the Gazette, Autumn 1979

Just as the acquisition of the Sloane Street premises after the war fulfilled the Corps' needs at that time, so its surrender twenty years later proved, in the long run, a blessing. It meant the loss of the Club, but by 1967 that did not seem as serious as it would have done say, ten years earlier; in any case, the FANYs were able to join the Service Women's Club, and later on to become members of the Special Forces Club – the only women to be granted that privilege. As for a headquarters, in November 1967 the Corps found a new home within the Duke of York's Headquarters in Chelsea.

Besides housing a number of well-disposed TAVR units, notably the SAS (Artists' Rifles) and the London Irish, the Duke of York's has a very comfortable, even rather grand, Officers' Mess, an ideal place for making those contacts which so often supplement, or circumvent, the more formal rituals of official application and submission. Another of the Duke of York's outstanding merits is space: space to train – those green figures cowering in the lee of the buildings on blustery winter evenings are FANYs doing an RT exercise! – and space in which to keep a vehicle. The Corps' Diamond Jubilee Year, 1967, besides being marked by a Service of Thanksgiving in the Household Brigade's jealously guarded chapel in Wellington Barracks, and a cocktail party in Chelsea Royal Hospital, among other things, was marked also by the more prosaic, but ultimately more useful, acquisition of a minibus. It was bought by means of a raffle, and opened up all sorts of possibilities for training, not only in driving and map-reading, but in radio work; indeed, it made possible the creation of the Mobile Communication Unit (MCU), which was to lead to some of the Corps' most interesting assignments in the years ahead. In common with a number of things that happened in those last years of the 1960s, the minibus was a symbol of a change of fortune, the result of firm and vigorous direction from the top and, in consequence, a new sense of purpose throughout the Corps.

The 1967 Camp, or Annual Training Week, was held under canvas in Wales, for a change, and included map reading and some RT. This was to become an increasingly important part of the FANYs' armoury of skills, for it tied in with the developing idea of the Mobile Communication Unit. The van, fitted with a powerful aerial, was able to act as network control for any number of girls in different places with *their* sets. Time and training were needed before this was able to be applied to the full: meanwhile practice was provided at the British Horse Society's Trials and the Courage Trophy. More of that later; but it is one of the pointers towards the present day.

The other innovation, originally suggested in broad terms by MacLellan after the war, but not taken up until 1969, was the formation of a language group. The Corps possessed a number of fluent linguists – by the autumn the group could produce a dozen different tongues – and it seemed a pity not to put them to use. From the start two basic rules were established: they were not out to compete with professional interpreters, and they would be completely non-political. Apart from that, they would be prepared to help any visiting group of foreigners who needed them; and they were perfectly right in thinking that, when the word got round, they would not lack for customers. The group, as lively as they are multilingual, is still going strong: we shall meet them again later.

The Corps' activities are divided, essentially, into those which are compulsory – its raison d'être – and those which are voluntary, a kind of reward or perk. Communications in all its ramifications, first aid, and certain introductory lectures for newly joined members – Corps history, for example – come into the first category: rifle-shooting and unarmed combat, now known as close-quarters battle, come into the second. Between the two there are a number of things, like attendance at Camp or horse trials, which are not exactly compulsory, but which members are encouraged to attend. As Grace Ashley Smith said at the beginning, the Corps is for workers, not shirkers; or as Sheila Parkinson puts it, it is not a social club, nor is it a cure for loneliness. It would make a good model for any society, if human nature were not such a perverse and awkward little number.

Suggestions for either category, work or 'play', are always welcome and, when possible, evaluated in practice. One led to the girls having the chance to strip down, reassemble and fire a variety of current light weapons: another, being investigated, is parachuting. It has not proved possible to meet yet another suggestion, that they should learn to drive a tank. But as one girl remarked, 'A friend said that she would like to learn unarmed combat. "Oh, I'm doing that in the FANYs," I said. The same with Morse, shooting, map-reading – I've learnt them all in the FANYs.'

ii

> 'As we were driven by coach to Dachau, my mind went back to a September day twenty-five years before when I had escaped with another FANY, Blanche Charlet, and fifty men from the dreadful prison at Castres ... Many ghosts were standing beside me during the very moving Memorial Service, as several of my friends died quite horribly in various camps and prisons.'
> Suzanne Charisse, at the unveiling of the Memorial at Dachau, September 1968

> 'Our aim is to offer a constructive voluntary service in the field of communications, both from a technical and language aspect, a combination not provided at the present time by any other voluntary organization.'
> Sheila Parkinson in the Gazette, Spring 1969

The Corps' identification with SOE, and especially with its women agents, runs, a grim and golden thread, through its post-war history. In the autumn of 1968 a memorial was unveiled at Dachau to those thousands who had died within its hellish confines, among them the four FANYs, Yolande Beekman, Madeleine Damerment, Noor Inayat Khan and Eliane Plewman. In the British party that attended that day were Major-General Sir Colin Gubbins, representing SOE, and Sheila Parkinson and Suzanne Charisse, who laid a wreath on behalf of the FANY. Suzanne had been closely involved in the running of two escape routes for Allied airmen shot down over Europe. Captured, interrogated, tortured and condemned to three months solitary confinement in 1942, she was eventually released – and promptly joined another network, conducting fugitives from Paris to Marseilles. She was captured a second time, and condemned to death in a prison near Toulouse; but, as she says above, escaped in a mass break-out in the nick of time. Seven years after the Dachau ceremony Sheila Parkinson, accompanied by Joan Drummond and Margaret Butler-Wright, attended an equally sombre occasion at Natzweiler, of equally vile repute, where Andrée Borrel, Vera Leigh and Diana Rowden were murdered. The FANY connection with SOE, imperfectly recognized even by those with some knowledge of the work of the 'Baker Street Irregulars', forms an imperishable garland in the FANY's corporate memory.

By the 1970s the various ideas for giving the Corps a useful and coherent role were beginning to take shape. As early as 1968 the CO had been in touch with the Metropolitan and City of London Police about the possible contribution of the MCU in various emergencies, and a number of regional police forces showed interest as well. There were two obstacles to be overcome: one, the limited resources, financial and numerical, of the Corps; the other the organizational difficulty of slotting such a voluntary effort into the structure of a police force; and it took time to resolve them. In the meantime members of the Corps could train so that when they were resolved, they were ready to assume any new duties that came their way – an application of Princess Alice's dictum of 'continuous training' and 'preparedness', combined with MacLellan's emphasis on 'specialized skills'. In fact, from 1969 onwards the 'Bus Unit', as it was then known, was on call in case of a major disaster in the Greater London area; but it was not fully integrated into the police system until later.

After attending an exercise at Northolt in 1971 – the 'incident' was a realistically staged aircraft crash – one of the girls described the

Casualty Bureau set up by the police, and wrote prophetically: 'The Corps Mobile Unit, with its own frequency, could make a valuable contribution here, by providing a link between hospital, casualty bureau and incident post, and dealing with documentation in its entirety, thus releasing policemen and telephone lines for other work.' Three years later the Unit was being included in the *Major Incident Manuals* of both forces, and was soon to be involved in a very major incident indeed.

'It has been a year,' Sheila Parkinson wrote in the *Gazette* in September 1970, 'spent consolidating our present activities; and doing all we can from HQ to make them known.' And that autumn she started to put advertisements inviting recruits in the national press, which pulled in a number of suitable applicants: this was to become a regular thing.

FANY participation in horse trials has already been mentioned. The British Horse Society holds trials on various courses throughout the south of England between spring and autumn. These cross-country events involve numerous jumps, water-splashes and other hazards, and falls are not unknown. With FANYs manning RT sets at strategic points and in touch with network control at the event HQ, the result of the competitors' performance can be transmitted instantly, thus keeping the scoreboard updated, and officials apprised of an accident. Similar demands are made on those who attend the Courage Trophy. This is an annual jamboree, sponsored by the brewers, in which thirty or more teams from the London branches of the TAVR take part in two days of competitions which range from assault course to first aid, and shooting to anti-ambush. The FANYs' job is to keep a tally of the scores of each event – they take place all over the country-side round Camberley – and radio them to Stats Control at Pirbright, who pass them on to the keepers of the scoreboard at Duke of York's HQ. In the seven years in which they have been doing it, the FANYs have notched up an unbroken record of never having got a result wrong.

Activities of this kind, halfway between work and play, help to keep wits sharp and radio skills furbished, but out of the classroom. This is essential because at the end of 1973 arrangements were finally tied up with the City of London Police for the FANYs to be on call in the event of a disaster within 'the Square Mile' of their manor. What this means in practice is that every active member of the Corps is bound to attend two Documentation sessions a year in the Central Casualty and Inquiry Bureau (CCB) on the seventh floor of the Bishopsgate Police Station, and to be prepared to turn out at any time of the day or night if summoned. This does not mean that the hundred or so trained girls have to spend their lives within earshot of a telephone; but out of that number there will always be the fourteen – seven teams of two – required who are. Documentation training started in earnest in 1973, and the following year the teams were fully operational.

The vital link between the police and the teams is a list of six FANYs who are normally at home and who have the phone numbers of everyone involved, including the CO. Told of an emergency, the one to get the message rings round until she has the fourteen lined up. 'This is a police call-out by the City Police. Can you report to head-quarters immediately?' The first girl to reach HQ fills in the details in the logbook and, as soon as she has a team-mate, hares off to Bishopsgate. The others, pausing only to pick up their RT sets, go as directed, either to the scene of the disaster or to one of the three city hospitals, the London, Guy's or Barts. Within sixty to ninety minutes, night or day, during office hours or not, the seven teams will be at their stations.

Their job is this. Whenever there is a serious incident, a telephone number is usually broadcast on radio and television, and people who think relatives or friends may be involved start ringing the police for information. At the same time, details about casualties are coming in from the scene by RT, telephone or despatch rider. The FANYs in the CCB at their telephones and RT sets deal with both sides: recording names and details of the presumed victims on the one hand; and on the other, names and details, where possible, of the actual casualties, and matching the two through display boards and appropriate forms. They should, therefore, be able to tell the inquirer that, yes, her husband was involved, is injured, and has been taken to Barts; or that, no, no one of that name and description has been reported. During the training sessions such a situation is convincingly simulated under the eye of a Chief Inspector. One Friday in February 1975, however, it was the real thing.

iii

*'The Documentation team handled over eight hundred
calls during Friday night – reliefs were sent up on
Saturday morning and they worked at top pressure...
The first telephone inquiries were completely lucid, then,
as people began to realize that perhaps their friends or relatives were involved, it became increasingly difficult to
acquire coherent information.'*

Gazette, Spring 1975

It was Friday, February 28th, 1975. That evening, an underground
train travelling from Islington ran, for reasons which have never been
established, full tilt into the buffers at Moorgate station, with horren-
dous results. It was the first time that the FANYs were called out on a
real emergency. The article quoted above gives some idea of what
that neutral term 'Documentation' can actually mean; it goes on:

'Within one hour of call-out, the first RT team arrived at Barts, closely
followed by second and third teams which went immediately to the
London and Guy's hospitals. The first team was redirected to the scene
of the incident and the third team to Bishopsgate Police Station and
maintained a net for police administrative messages all that afternoon.
They were also instrumental in relaying messages to and from the
London Hospital. Subsequently, after all living casualties had been
rescued, the first RT team withdrew to augment the Documentation
team at Bishopsgate Police Station where they were joined by the second
team. Work proceeded throughout Friday night and continued without
a break until the final team left Bishopsgate at 20.00 hours on the following Tuesday...

'The first night was emotionally as well as physically exhausting. It
was a revelation to discover that in such appalling circumstances people
actually telephoned in with "loaded" questions and hoax calls... Of
course there were graphic moments. Mental pictures emerged of sheer
relief at the other end of the telephone that somebody's close relative
was safe; the obvious agony of anxious parents... At the Casualty
Bureau the scene was one of quiet efficiency. Everyone knew exactly
what she was doing and we were accepted as an integral part of their organization, and although our part there was played in comparative
comfort, the thoughts were always with those actually involved in the
grim rescue operations.

'At the scene of the disaster our two RT operations were too busy to
appreciate in full the horror of the situation not twenty yards from their
car... Visions of exhausted firemen with blackened faces, canister

after canister of oxygen, heavy lifting equipment ... a young Salvation Army girl being quietly sick while she rested and, slightly apart from the rest of us, the mother of the WPC sitting in the white police car, tensely awaiting news of her daughter ...'

There has not been a comparable disaster within the City of London since, but Moorgate, so shattering in its unexpectedness, so appalling in its results, stands as a reminder that such calamities can and, on occasion, do happen.

Another duty that the Corps undertook in the 1970s was to provide a radio link between Tower Hamlets and the Isle of Dogs in the event of the Thames overflowing its banks and, according to prediction, flooding the lower-lying boroughs of London to a depth of fifteen feet or more. This particular disaster, in which no one quite believed, did not happen, though there were a number of alerts during the years that the flood barrier was being built, and in 1978 the margin at the Embankment at one high water was ten inches. On February 1st, 1983 – three years later, and many millions of pounds dearer than estimated – the barrier, looking like a row of miniature Sydney Opera Houses, was raised for the first time, and the teams were able to stand down.

But disaster can strike at any time: aircraft crash, trains come off the rails or collide, homicidal maniacs secrete bombs in busy shopping streets. Will there always be someone else to tend the injured, comfort the bereaved, and clear up the mess? The FANYs work on the conviction that, where their particular skills apply, they should be the 'someone else'.

iv

'The following languages are available: French, Italian, German, Spanish, Norwegian, Russian, Polish, Japanese, Swahili, Arabic.'

Gazette, Spring 1973

Imagine, if you can, a Conference of Basketball Referees, a bevy of Italian Women Footballers, or the Twenty-first World Conference on Social Welfare attended by representatives from sixty-four countries, or the delegation to the Inter-Parliamentary Union from Gabon which has forty-eight languages in daily use within its modest frontiers (though luckily the members of the delegation spoke French). And having conjured up one or more of these improbable gatherings, imagine being thrown into them and having to calm them, shepherd them here and there, and explain to them in any language they can understand the operation of the British system of licensing laws or the workings of a Select Committee of the House of Commons. The mind of the average monoglot pops like a blown fuse at the very thought of such jabbering babels: the members of the FANY Language Group take them in their interpretative stride.

It took some time for the Group to make its existence known to the kinds of organization that have need of such skills; but once known, they were much in demand, and many a party of Japanese ping-pong players and Filipino canoeists and Algerian parliamentarians might have been lost without trace had it not been for the Group's patient guidance.

Much of the credit for the Group's popularity must be given to Frances Humphery, the Deputy Corps Commander. Mrs Humphery, who claims ironically but with perfect truth not to have a drop of British blood in her veins – she is Austrian by birth and English by marriage – arrived in Britain in 1938 and tried to join the FANY but was turned down. Thirty-five years later and widowed, she applied again, and two years later was appointed deputy to the CO. As she speaks English, French and German with equal fluency, it was inevitable that she should also take over the Language Group. The standards that she imposes on applicants – and forty answered one advertisement in the Press – are strict. No nonsense about O-Level French: a high conversational level is required, and, since the Group undertakes some translation as well, a reasonable level of literacy. The Group, some of whose members also take part in normal Corps activities, is one of its success stories, though probably little known outside circles that have to deal with visiting delegations: among them, its stock stands high.

During the 1970s the names of several members who have figured in these pages had to be added to the list of members past. Pat Beauchamp Washington (née Waddell), one of the Corps' most vigorous and vocal members since before the First World War, died at

Christmas 1972. Cole-Hamilton died the following year; so did Hope Gamwell and Phyllis Bingham; and the year after, Dicky Runciman of the Finnish débâcle, and Winifred Mason, OBE, who had taken over the SOE Units from Bingham. In 1976 Major-General Sir Colin Gubbins, who had been a member of the Advisory Council since the war, and of whom it was said that 'he deserved more of his country than he ever received'; and in 1977 two former COs, Marian Gamwell and Maud MacLellan.

The tributes to the latter two were effusive and sincere for, in their different ways, they were both women of stature. But whereas Maud MacLellan was a delightful person and an admirable and dedicated commanding officer, the Gamwell sisters with their bush-whacking in East Africa and their parallel devotion to the Corps were unique. Marian especially was made in the mould of women like Mary Kingsley, untrammelled by the conventional thinking of lesser mortals: on one of her wartime trips, needing to get to Baghdad, and with no other transport available, she seriously suggested that she might take a camel!

And 1977, that year of conflicting emotions, held other events worthy of record. It was, for one thing, the Corps' Seventieth Anniversary as well as being the Queen's Silver Jubilee Year, and the Corps took as a particularly favourable omen the award, in the Jubilee Honours list, of an OBE to their CO. This was certainly worth a party, and one was duly held to celebrate it in the Headquarters Mess on December 10th. Princess Alice, seventeen years older than the Corps but with her affection for 'her' FANYs undimmed, received a birthday visit from ten of them, dressed in the various uniforms of the seven decades, and asked them all in for a sherry and a yarn. She also attended the annual reunion and, on a freezing November day, the memorial service to MacLellan and Gamwell. Few organizations can have had a more loyal, indomitable – or, indeed, indestructible – Royal patron.

In 1969 Sheila Parkinson, as quoted at the head of a previous section, had clearly seen communications as the Corps' most fruitful role for the future, and the links established with the City of London Police seemed to justify this view. It was confirmed in 1980 when, as she reported in the *Gazette*, 'A senior Officer from the Royal Corps of

Signals came to see us, to find out if we could provide urgently needed support in their small Army Communications Centres in the United Kingdom during times of tension or National Emergency when it became necessary to operate twenty-four hours a day.' Over the next three years the scheme was worked out in detail; and in 1983 the Corps, its integrity and professionalism vouched for by General Charles Page (its Honorary Colonel and himself a signaller), was given official recognition – for the first time since 1947.

Not a lot can be said about the work since it is confidential, but in essentials it is this. The Army in Britain has a complex and sophisticated signals network linking its numerous establishments throughout the kingdom by teleprinter. The permanent staff at these communications centres, both civilians and members of the Royal Corps of Signals, can handle normal traffic; but in a crisis they need extra, trained hands. The job is both responsible and exacting, and the fact that the Corps was asked to undertake it was taken as a tribute to their efficiency.

In due course FANY members signed the Official Secrets Act and began to take part in training sessions at 'Com-Cens', as they are called, in south-east England. Once trained, they do three refresher courses a year.

The Com-Cens are discreet, anonymous little buildings in military establishments, subject to extremely tight security and virtually unknown except to those directly involved. No one else ever enters them; even signals for despatch are handed in through a hatch. Within these forbidding and windowless walls the strictest signals procedures are enforced – the Manual is as thick as a telephone directory – and speed, accuracy and total obedience to the rules as laid down are *de rigeur*. 'Once you have grasped the logic of the system,' one of the girls said with a hint of resignation, 'it begins to make sense'; but to master that logic is by no means easy. The regular staff do a three-months intensive course to qualify: the FANYs are expected to become at least usefully proficient with a short course of lectures and a couple of training sessions.

Sitting in a rather stuffy concrete box for eight hours, wrestling with the complexities of military methods, military jargon, and the seemingly impenetrable jungle of Army addresses and their locations around the world, under the unforgiving eye of the Supervisor – and without pay – is not everyone's idea of the way to spend a jolly

Saturday afternoon, but the FANYs seem to enjoy it, just as they enjoy the Documentation sessions at Bishopgate.

To accept that they do enjoy their work is essential to an understanding of the Corps, and the reason why it has survived for nearly a hundred years. The urge to be of use is strong in many people, but in times of relative peace and prosperity it is not easily fufilled. The FANY taps that idealism at its source, and that is where its strenght lies.

With the death of Princess Alice in the spring of 1981, a long chapter in the history of the FANY was closed. Her loyalty and enthusiasm had never waned. She had been a wise, steadfast and affectionate friend for nearly half a century, and she had been greatly loved and honoured in return. And there were other reminders of time passing in those years: the death of Beryl Hutchinson in the same year, and of the veteran of them all, Tony Colston – 100 years old – in 1982. With their passing went the last living links with the old, brave, insouciant days. The world had changed almost beyond recognition since then, and the FANY had changed with it.

15

Continuity Through Change
1984–2003
I · THE MILITARY COMMITMENT

'The Hercules flew over the DZs at about 800 feet with the side door open so we could peer out into the darkness and see the moonlight reflected on the flat areas of water . . . It was cold – 5° on the ground. We watched as the small teams of parachutists left the plane. After hurtling down the runway it stopped briefly to disgorge the rest of us and our kit onto the tarmac. The only lights were the headlights of the vehicles coming to meet us – no passport control or customs. We grabbed our kit and ran towards the vehicles and the plane roared off . . .'

Veronica Gates, on exercise with a
TA regiment in northern Europe

Following Sheila Parkinson's shrewd appreciation of the opportunities open to the Corps and the limitations imposed on it in the problematic conditions of the 1980s, it became smaller, more specialized and more professional. The technological demands of a society increasingly dominated by the silicon chip, satellite and computer left little scope for the enthusiastic amateur, however competent and well intentioned.

By 1984 the Corps was reflecting this downsized role. It had become concentrated around its HQ at the Duke of York's Headquarters in London, where it had now had its home for 15 years, and where – at least for the time being – its tenure appeared to be secure. The FANY commitment to augment the Army Communications

Centres in a national emergency strengthened its foothold in the Duke of York's, as did an invitation to join the TAVR Association for Greater London as a co-opted member – a true compliment for so unorthodox an organization! Yet while the twice-yearly *Gazette* no longer carried a section entitled 'News of the London FANYs', there being practically no active FANYs *but* London ones, the training programme was as varied and interesting as ever. Frustratingly perhaps, the greatest changes taking place within the Corps were those that could not be advertised, since they involved closer work with Special Forces and secure army units. Through a combination of personal recommendation, contacts and an established reputation for sound common sense and reliability, the Corps was gradually strengthening its links with the Territorial and Regular Armies – but doing so very much behind the scenes.

These efforts bore fruit. From the mid-1980s Joint Services exercises became a growing part of the training programme. FANYs trained with the Parachute Regiment in such far-flung places as Benbecula in the Western Isles. In February 1987 ten FANYs took part in the WINTEX NATO Exercise. Six of them, working in shifts, suddenly found that the exercise had become real when they had the chilling task of passing messages on the sinking of the *Herald of Free Enterprise*. It was a lesson, frequently repeated by 'old hands' but learned only through experience by new recruits, that the need for training is often routine and unexciting, yet gives the skills required to be of immediate use in a disaster.

On 16 January 1991, as well as being called on to run an Army COMCEN, the FANY responded to a call for volunteers to man MOD Casualty Bureaux following the outbreak of the Gulf War – a theatre of battle that during the Cold War era would have seemed wholly unlikely. The Corps was asked to support the Army in the receipt and passage of information on casualties of the hostilities in the Gulf and in their allocation and dispersal to hospitals throughout the UK. The casualty cell, which operated 'somewhere in West London', as the *Daily Telegraph* put it, was manned day and night by a team of 36 working in shifts,who answered calls made through 17 telephone lines specially laid on for the operation. It was the first time the Army had provided such an information service. It had done so in response to criticism of MOD after the Falklands conflict, when relatives of service personnel felt that they had not had access

to sufficient information on casualties. This was particularly important during the Gulf War, given the extraordinary media coverage
of the conflict, especially by Cable News Network (CNN). It was
therefore a vital link in ensuring that relatives were unlikely to learn
of casualties before they were informed by the relevant military
authorities.

In 1999 the Corps took part in an exercise at RAF Chicksands to
practice planning, deployment and operations in a short-warning
scenario of the UK Joint Force within a multinational environment.
The exercise, which cost £2 million and involved 700 participants
from all three services, presented a complex scenario of ethnic
conflicts, oil deposits, fisheries' disputes and political unrest.

By now, participation in exercises with TA Royal Signals regiments was a regular part of the FANY training calendar. Each
September the annual major signals exercise involves the FANY in a
variety of roles; from supervising signal stations in the UK and overseas to impersonating panic-stricken members of the civilian
population, importunate journalists and fifth columnists. While
immensely enjoyable and nurturing the acting skills of many an
embryonic thespian, these exercises are also a crucial part of training
for both peace and wartime situations.

In October 1999 the Corps joined 1 (RBY) Signal Squadron on
the annual training exercise in Denmark. That year's exercise, codenamed 'Runnel Stone', was designed to test the squadron's combat
ability and the capacities of the Danish Home Defence Force in the
face of a more unorthodox enemy! The FANYs assisted in their time-
honoured way, coding and uncoding messages, caching bombs,
hiding in deserted houses and acting as conductors for illegal partisans. They also marked out a drop zone at night with infra-red
torches, waiting for the Hercules to surge out of the darkness before
retrieving the dropped ammunition and dragging it to safety. The
value the TA places on the Corps' input into this training, which
also includes radio communications and an impressive range of
language skills, was reflected in the decision in 2001 by 2 (National
Communications) Signal Brigade to give the FANY a formal role in
its ORBAT (Order of Battle). Relevant training is with 71
(Yeomanry) Signal Regiment, and contacts with the Brigade have
opened up opportunities to establish links with a range of specialist
groups. There is a symbolic as well as a historic appropriateness to

this, in that the FANY and the Royal Corps of Signals share the same Colonel-in-Chief, The Princess Royal. There has long been a FANY section in the Museum of the Royal Corps of Signals at Blandford, where Corps members attend training from time to time. And in the mid-1990s, the Corps spent several weekends at Blandford, where they learned to use sophisticated lightweight radio systems, plan and direct exercises and set up a command post.

When the Berlin Wall came down on 9 November 1989, a group of FANYs were on a special communications exercise north of London. As they watched events unfold on television, they, along with many others, realized that the world – and their role in it – would irrevocably change. In the global realignment that followed, traditional enemies became potential allies, power bases shifted and the Western Alliance took up new challenges. As the events of 11 September 2001 spectacularly showed, the threat to peace is now less concentrated, the enemy more nebulous and volatile. While it would not be accurate to suggest that the political realignments in the world have led to a complete transformation of the FANYs' military training (any more than they have that of any of the reserve forces), nevertheless elements have crept in to reflect new roles and concerns. These have included an introduction to nuclear, biological and chemical warfare at the Guards Training Depot at Pirbright, involving immersion in a CS gas chamber and lectures on the full spectrum of lethal, damaging and incapacitating agents.

The proliferation of terrorist attacks around the world that has cast a shadow across the new millennium has also begun to blur the distinction between 'military' and 'civil' emergencies. Initially approached by the MOD to provide operations during the Gulf War, the FANY now assists the Army Crisis Coordination Cell in Upavon, Wiltshire, by running a complementary unit at the Headquarters of the Corps in London. In July 2000, the FANY was asked to provide support for 256 (City of London) Field Hospital, its neighbour at the Duke of York's Headquarters, in setting up a 50-bed hospital at the Farnborough Air Show. The FANYs' task was to run the documentation for an emergency disaster exercise – and of course to perform the same tasks 'live' if there were a real incident – true as ever to their motto 'I cope'.

ii   The Civil Responsibility

'The FANYs provided a vital support role to the entire police operation. Their speedy response and tireless dedication above and beyond the call of duty, was a lesson to us all.'

Inspector P. Gilbert, City of London Police,
following the St Mary Axe bombing, 10 April 1992

In the early hours of Friday 16 October 1987 hurricane-force winds ripped through the United Kingdom, causing extensive damage and disruption. In the City of London, a partly demolished tower block adjacent to the Barbican complex collapsed with its scaffolding, and nearby flats were evacuated when a large overhead crane appeared to be about to blow over. The call-out to FANYs to man the casualty bureau was taken by Marigold Blake-Hill (three of the other call-out operators' telephones were out of order). In pitch darkness, with the aid of a torch and using a public telephone, she and her husband rang 30 numbers, some of which were also out of order, and alerted 18 operators within 45 minutes. They got to the Bishopsgate Casualty Bureau in record time despite hazardous journeys, and the first FANYs – including the then DCC Miranda Gavin on the eve of her wedding – arrived 45 minutes after call-out. From then on both that Bureau and FANY HQ were manned with an RT team standing by in case it was needed. At 6.30 the FANYs had the only live telephone in the Duke of York's HQ, and it was liberally used by the Police and a TA unit. The office, with its gas fire and candles, became the centre of activity and the gas stove made it possible to provide tea and coffee until power was restored.

Four years later regular training paid off again when on 8 January 1991 the packed Sevenoaks to London commuter service ran into the buffers on platform 3 at Cannon Street station. There were around 1,000 passengers on board, many of whom were standing or preparing to leap from the train as it came to a halt. Two people died in the accident. Within an hour of the first 999 call the casualty bureau at Bishopsgate was up and running, staffed by 22 FANYs and City of London police – their first daytime call-out since the Moorgate disaster. Later that year, the Corps extended their emergency coverage by participating in Exercise 'Hammer', which simulated a head-on collision between two Hammersmith and City line trains on a viaduct between Ladbroke Grove and Latimer Road stations. It was the largest exercise ever mounted by London Underground, and the first time the FANYs had worked with them.

In 1992 and 1993 two huge IRA car bombs exploded in central London, the first at the Baltic Exchange in St Mary Axe, and the second at Bishopsgate itself, just yards from the city police Casualty Bureau. The attack on a building of international standing in the heart of the City of London brought with it its own specific challenges: over 3,000 calls poured in from anxious relatives and friends of city workers from as far afield as the United States and the Far East. Within minutes of the blast FANY volunteers were picking their way through broken glass and shattered concrete to the casualty bureau – some of them even having to sneak through police cordons to get there as quickly as possible since the entire area had been sectioned off.

The close association between the Corps and the City of London Police, which began in the early 1970s and was first successfully put to the test following the Moorgate crash in 1974, has continued unbroken. The views of the FANY operators, some of whom are now as experienced as many of the police, are always heeded. When they comment on procedures and suggest improvements to the system, these remarks are invariably implemented. The Corps can justifiably claim that they have shaped the way the Bureau is run. They have taken part in every major incident declared, including a call-out following the sinking of the *Marchioness* riverboat in August 1989 and the atrocity of 11 September 2001. Such incidents underline the conviction held by FANY members of the need to train and refresh continually.

One annual commitment is to have a team on standby for the Lord Mayor's Show day, when an accident or incident could quickly escalate into a disaster. For several years now, the CID have used this day for an exercise, using as a scenario an incident that was also a crime. In this way they have become aware of the FANY role in the Casualty Bureau and that the FANY were among the first to be consulted on the HOLMES system, a huge police database enquiry system for the CID. HOLMES 2, a new and powerful database system, was introduced in 1999 and FANYs were among the first to 'break it in' for use in documentation data entry. At the beginning of the new millennium the Corps has firmly established itself as a linchpin in the sphere of civil emergency communications.

iii   The Seasonal Round

'Training night became alive with enthusiastic members attending various activities, since recruits' training was running simultaneously . . . And so we await the set up and training for the Army Casualty Bureau, plan on a weekend in early summer to test the system, and after Camp it will be time to start work on the next exercise. Last year's recruits are in their teams and new recruits are ready to be trained – the cycle of the year continues to turn.'

Joan Drummond, Training Officer,
in her summary of the year's training (2000)

Obviously, civil emergency call-outs and military exercises are the high-water marks in a Corps calendar that, like the seasons, has its more prosaic – though gratifyingly familiar and comforting – regularities. The CO's start-of-the-year address in January, the Courage Trophy TA competition and language training in March, Annual Camp in May, the Open Day in July, the AGM and Reunion Cocktail Party (which has been held on the last Saturday in October since the 1920s), the Field of Remembrance at Westminster Abbey in November . . . all of these recur on an annual basis. Although, as any Corps member will tell you, no single event, including those that come round each year, is ever the same twice! Some events at which FANY attendance has been *de rigueur* have sadly disappeared from the annual round. The Hampton Sponsored Ride in Surrey was held for the last time in 2000, though FANYs are occasionally on duty at the Windsor Horse Trials, and the Royal Tournament, where the FANYs first appeared in 1909, has fallen victim to the defence spending cutbacks.

Happily though, Corps members in service dress are still a regular sight as they collect for the Army Benevolent Fund at the Chelsea Flower Show each year. And then there are the many

Remembrance events in which the FANY regularly participates. In 1990 FANY and FANY ATS veterans resumed their places in the service and march past the Cenotaph after an absence of many years, and this has now become a permanent feature in the Corps calendar. A FANY regularly appears in dress uniform at the British Legion's Festival of Remembrance at the Royal Albert Hall. There is the Kensington & Chelsea Parade, in which the Corps became involved after one of their number became Mayor*. As members of the City of London RFCA, the FANY is also represented at the wreath-laying ceremony at the Royal Exchange. And finally, there is the Corps' own private ceremony at their 'home' church of St Paul's, Knightsbridge, when each year the names of their war dead are read out.

Inevitably, though, a Corps history is defined more by red-letter days than by routine. Those that have marked the past two decades reflect the uniqueness of the FANY. In 1987 the Corps reached another key anniversary: its 80th year of continuous service, a longevity unequalled by any other voluntary organization for women. The commemoration service at the Guards Chapel was attended, as always, by representatives of the French and Belgian governments. At a time when other women's units – few enough already – the WRNS, WRAC and WAAF – were either being merged or disbanded, the FANYs' hybrid nature ensured its survival. That, and its ability subtly to adapt itself to the latest exigencies.

1994 was a red-letter year: the bicentennial of the founding of the first Yeomanry units, raised to defend Britain during the Napoleonic wars. The FANY – the only women's unit to bear the title 'Yeomanry' – was invited to participate in the Year of the Yeomanry. As part of the celebrations, The Queen reviewed all the Yeomanry units in Windsor Great Park on 17 April. The Corps was represented by Vivienne Williams in the dashing scarlet, blue and white 1907 dress uniform, but with a cleverly adapted skirt, as she had sensibly refused to ride an unfamiliar horse side-saddle! A contingent of uniformed FANYs led the parade onto the arena. The Queen herself, of course, has other, more personal links with the Corps, having

---

*The FANY have provided two Mayors: Elizabeth Christmas, who was twice elected Mayor of Kensington and Chelsea, and Frances Blois, who became Lord Mayor of Westminster in 2002.

attended a motor driving course in 1945 at No. 1 MT Training Centre, Camberley as Princess Elizabeth.

1994 also saw an historic return by the FANY to horseback, when they were invited to provide a team for the Honourable Artillery Company's Uniformed Services (later the Inter-Services) Jumping Championships. This competition, held annually at the riding school of the King's Troop, Royal Horse Artillery in St John's Wood, attracts riders from the Reserve Forces the world over. Since that first foray into the world of competitive show jumping, the FANY team has carried off the cup several times, taken the prize for Best Lady Rider and supplemented these honours by winning their colours abroad at the Reserve Forces show-jumping competition in Saumur, France. The Corps' beginnings as a mounted unit and its reputation for producing fine horsewomen has resulted in close links with the Farriers Company, which donated the silver cup that is presented each year to the best new FANY recruit.

The closer links with the Regular and Reserve Forces mentioned earlier are also reflected in other aspects of Corps activities. In the late 1980s the FANY language section began military language training with the Joint Services Interrogation Organization, and later with 22 Intelligence Company (V) at the Defence School of Languages at Beaconsfield. This provides members with intensive linguistic training from beginner to interpreter level in a wide range of languages and allows them to take a series of military qualifications. The Corps also supplies language skills to a variety of military and civilian 'clients'; Italian translators for an exercise in Sicily with the Parachute Regiment, pre-exercise briefing in Arabic and Middle Eastern customs for specialist signals squadrons, translation into English of the proceedings of the Bologna conference on the SOE in Italy, interpreters for the Inter-Parliamentary Union Group. In July 1998 the NATO Reserve Forces Congress asked the Section to provide translators in several languages – this eventually involved several members acting as guides to the delegates on a whistle-stop tour of London! The reunification of Germany, the Gulf War and the break-up of the Soviet Union have dramatically changed the services' linguistic requirements, however. German and Russian have slid down the list of priorities and there has been an upsurge in demand for Arabic. Many Corps members have signed up for this immensely difficult language, and the pace of the classes is reported to be hard and fast. There are moments of light relief, however. During a break, one of the Arabic tutors famously produced an Egyptian phrasebook for the Edwardian traveller ("Boatman, use the oars a little faster but if you splash us with water it will be the worse for you!")*.

And finally, the annual training camp remained (and indeed remains) the most important weekend in the FANY calendar, being the only event that combines all the skills for which the Corps is known (and therefore subject to a three-line whip!). However, by the 1980s it had been truncated to a long Bank Holiday weekend in May in recognition of the increased professional and family commitments of its members. It had also been somewhat peripatetic, relocating from Crowborough in Sussex (1984) to St Martin's Plain, Shorncliffe near Dover (1985) and back to Crowborough again before finally re-establishing itself at Longmoor in Hampshire in 1991. Since then, all annual camps have been held there – the TA's main training area – again reflecting the Corps' closer links with the Army. Only in 2001 were activities temporarily switched to London following the closure of many rural training sites in the wake of the national outbreak of foot and mouth disease. Training activities now regularly include navigation and orienteering, shooting (one FANY is a fully qualified range instructor), survival techniques, Life Saver and Life Saver Plus first aid training and work with the Royal Corps of Signals. As always, hard work is laced with the ever-present ingredients of fun, laughter, friendship and shared endeavour.

iv   The Illustrious Memory

'In years to come I can visualise young people looking at this plaque and asking their parents "Who was Odette and what did she do to get the George Cross?" I hope the answer will be that, although she regarded herself as a very ordinary person, she possessed that rarest of all human virtues – indomitable courage . . . Her example should be an

---

*Among the languages currently spoken by the Corps are: Arabic, Chinese (Putongwa and Mandarin), Dutch, French, Fiji, German, Gujarati, Greek, Hindi, Hungarian, Italian, Polish, Portuguese, Punjabi, Russian, Serbo-Croat, Spanish, Swedish, Turkish.

*inspiration to those of us whose turn it is to maintain the
honour and reputation of the FANYs and this plaque to her
memory should remind us, and future generations, of the
nobility of which the human spirit is possible'*
*Major-General Patrick MacLellan, Chairman of the
Advisory Council, at the unveiling of the memorial to
Odette Hallowes, St Paul's Church Knightsbridge*

At no time during the last two decades have FANYs neglected to
remember those who went before them. The advent of anniver-
saries, the commemoration of founders, the acknowledgement of
sacrifice and bravery, and, inevitably, the passing of much-loved
veterans, friends and Corps mainstays have continued to punctuate
its narrative.

In 1991 The Queen Mother dedicated a large memorial at
Valençay to the memory of the 104 agents, seven of them FANYs, of
F Section Special Operations Executive, who died working with
the French Resistance. Vast and sentinel-like, it comprises two
columns, one black to symbolize night and the essential secrecy
of the operations, the other white to represent the shining spirit of
resistance which eventually triumphed.

Two years later Sadie Bonnell, the first FANY to be awarded the
Military Medal (and the first of the ten FANYs of the St Omer Convoy
personally decorated in the field by General Sir Herbert Plumer in
July 1918) died at the age of 105. In the same year, Corps
Commander Anna Whitehead led a group of FANYs on a visit to
Ravensbrück concentration camp, where a plaque was unveiled in
memory of Violette Szabo, Lilian Rolfe, Andrée Borrel and Cecily
Lefort. Odette Hallowes, undoubtedly the most famous surviving
FANY and a Vice-President of the Corps from 1967, saw the camp
where she had been a prisoner for the first time since her release.
Odette died in 1995 and is commemorated on a plaque next to the
FANY war memorial at St Paul's Knightsbridge, where every year she
had come to remember her fellow SOE agents who did not survive.

Four years later another small plaque was added in memory of
Eveline Fidgeon Shaw. Shaw was the only FANY lost on active service
during World War I, dying of dysentery while on duty as an ambulance driver near Sézanne. In 1997, to mark the 90th anniversary of
the founding of the Corps and to acquaint members with the

countries and circumstances in which their predecessors had worked, two trips were arranged to Flanders. One was a tour by coach of several of the World War One sites, including the first hospital at Lamarck in Calais. The second took the form of a navigation exercise involving the location of World War I camps, hospitals and casualty stations from original photos and documents. The two groups joined up at the weekend for a ceremony under the Menin Gate in Ypres, accompanied by men of the Belgian Army. The following day at a service at St George's Memorial Church, a plaque in honour of the FANYs who served on the Western Front was unveiled. A similar exercise was organized in 1998 centred on eastern France, where FANYs had served as ambulance drivers in the Bar-le-Duc and Nancy area. Their story – and the rigorous conditions under which they served – is beautifully recounted in *The Happy Foreigner*, a novel by the writer Enid Bagnold (author of *National Velvet*), who was herself a FANY driver in Alsace-Lorraine. The grave of Eveline Shaw, who was buried with full military honours by the French, was located and a short service held.

However, the commemorative highlight of the mid-1990s was undoubtedly the 50th anniversary of the final stages of World War Two. Wartime veterans and current active members played a full part in the various ceremonial occasions staged in London and in other parts of the British Isles. June 1944 saw a retrospective of D-Day and the preparations for the Normandy landings. Southwick House in Hampshire, formerly the headquarters of SHAEF, opened its doors to veterans to view the Overlord plans and to celebrate the Allied masterstroke at a garden party in the grounds.

In May 1995 the thoughts of the nation turned to VE Day, and the Corps had representatives at all the major commemorative events. A presentation to The Queen by both Houses of Parliament at Westminster Hall was the prelude to the opening ceremony of the VE events in Hyde Park, where Nancy Wake* was the FANY guest in the Royal Box. A contingent of World War II veterans paraded with the Corps flag and was later reviewed by the Royal Family in the forecourt of Buckingham Palace. The then Commanding

---

*Nancy Wake, an Australian FANY, became an SOE saboteur, organizer and Resistance fighter in France, leading an army of 7,000 Maquis troops in guerrilla warfare. She is the most highly decorated Allied servicewoman of World War II.

Officer, Anna Whitehead, later attended a reception and banquet for visiting heads of State at Guildhall and was joined by other FANY guests at the VE Service at St Paul's Cathedral.

August 1995 was a time for reflection on VJ Day and the some-times-forgotten campaign in the Far East. The Tribute and Promise Service outside Buckingham Palace took place in appropriately searing heat: typically undaunted, 23 FANY veterans joined the massive contingents marching down the Mall past The Queen. FANYs also attended receptions on the Royal Yacht and at the Tower of London, from which vantage points they watched the fly-past and firework display. VJ events in London ended with a magnificent and highly moving Beating Retreat and Sunset Ceremony on Horseguards Parade. Parallel events at Canterbury, Oxford, Romsey and Beverley, and in Scotland, Wales and Northern Ireland, were attended by locally-based FANYs. Although the em-phasis of these events was on commemoration and remembrance, there was an opportunity to look to the future by making use of the Unit Centres in Hyde Park (VE) and the Queen Elizabeth II Conference Centre (VJ), where information on the continuing work of the Corps, and recruitment material, was available for visitors.

Down the years the Corps has also been included in other commemorative events at which the history of their involvement is known only to the few – every one of these 'appearances' tells a fasci-nating story. Two former Polish Unit FANYs attended the unveiling of a statue to General Sikorski by The Duke of Kent at Portland Place in 2001. The general, killed in 1943, had Corps members among the Guard of Honour at his funeral. Relations with the Poles in exile have remained close over the years: there is a FANY uniform in the Polish Museum in London. Also in 2001, contingent was present (together with numerous Corps members who had come from all over the world) at a reception given at Beaulieu, one of the SOE training schools, to mark the 60th anniversary of the formation of SOE.

As the Corps moves into the new millennium, the honouring of those on whom it was founded and who have championed it continues. When the new *Dictionary of National Biography* appears in 2004 it will include several entries compiled by Lynette Beardwood, on nearly two dozen eminent FANYs, from Lilian Franklin, the first CO, to Maud MacLellan, who retired in 1964. The death on 18 May 2002 of Sheila Parkinson, the longest-serving

Corps Commander and the woman without whose tireless efforts the Corps might well have disbanded after the Second World War, came too late to be included in the new edition of the DNB, but will no doubt be added to the first appendix.

Later on in 2002, FANYs marked yet another milestone: the 60th anniversary of the parachuting into France of the first two FANY SOE agents, Andrée Borrel and Lise de Baissac. They landed at a drop zone at Bois Renard near Chambord in the Loire Valley, and were met on arrival by a reception committee that included a third FANY, Yvonne Rudellat. Of the three, only Lise de Baissac survived the war. In September 2002, on the anniversary of the drop, FANY members, assisted by Colonel Patrick Champenois and his Instructors from ETAP (the French Parachute School at Pau) returned to the area to re-enact the parachute landing. At a wreath-laying ceremony at Romorantin the following day the F Section FANYs were remembered for their bravery and sacrifice.

v   The New Horizon

'Their widely drawn constitution, which does not specify particular activities, makes the Corps as valuable today as it was in 1914 or 1939. Their spirit and qualities have in no way changed or diminished, and with their usual flexible outlook . . . they have during recent years developed strong ties with the City of London Police and the Royal Signals, where there are important roles for them in crisis management and communications in peacetime and wartime.'

Major-General Sir John Anderson,
FANY 80th Anniversary Thanksgiving Service

'Speaking on behalf of the SAS Regimental Association I can only say how indebted we are to the FANY . . . Due to your impending move, I am to be deprived of a much more interesting view – the comings and goings of many members of your Corps. You have brightened many dull and mundane moments – I will miss you as near neighbours.'

A member of the SAS, commenting on the
Corps' forthcoming move from E Block to
Mercury House in 1991

In addition to the steady march of events, the history of any organ-ization is also one of arrivals and departures. New names, fond farewells, fresh faces, sudden and abrupt truncations, painful re-adjustments, and, through it all, continuity under a different guise. The past 20 years have been no exception. In fact, it is also a truism that those who regret the passing of tradition have their equivalents in every age. However, in their defence, the past two decades have been exceptional in terms of changes *within* the FANY Corps (notwithstanding the upheavals caused by two world wars).

In 1990, after 25 years at the helm, Sheila Parkinson reluctantly stood down as Corps Commander. With her customary determi-nation, she told members that 'NOTHING but anno domini makes it necessary for me to relinquish this appointment'. Honor Irwin-Clark, the Adjutant and mainstay of the office, was a great help in the handover to Sheila Parkinson's successor, Anna Whitehead, the first CO to be recruited from outside the FANY fold. Despite this break with tradition, Mrs Whitehead's family background more than prepared her for the role she was about to assume. Her father, Lieutenant-Colonel Leonard Dismore, had joined SOE in 1941, and on his return to London had been attached to the Free French Section of SOE. Anna Whitehead, the wife of a naval officer, had travelled extensively and speaks fluent Portuguese and excellent French.

If Sheila Parkinson had presided over a new role for the Corps, Anna Whitehead's tenure saw the advent of other, perhaps more clearly visible, changes. The redesign of the FANY service dress was one. In the tradition of women's uniformed voluntary organiz-ations, skirts, shirts and jackets are handed down from older to younger members, and since the dress uniform has remained largely the same since the 1930s, its various constituent elements were bound to become progressively more worn – in every sense! Not only were linings frayed, but, to their dismay, 1990s recruits found that the anthropologists' claim that *homo sapiens* becomes larger with each successive generation was no lie. There was, however, a degree of consternation at HQ when the Peterborough column in *The Daily Telegraph* pronounced the FANYs to be 'busting out'.

Today, however, only the practised eye will detect the difference between the new-style service dress and its older companion, the main distinction being the use of bright red lining on the former. The Princess Royal wore the new-look uniform to officially open the Corps' new home of Mercury House in May 1993, a comparatively luxurious new accommodation block in the Duke of York's Headquarters, complete with an Axminster carpet in the Mess with the insignia and colours of the Corps woven into it. With the move to new premises came the revolution in updating office procedures, which began under Anna Whitehead with the acquisition of a couple of computers, a photocopier and a laptop. Plans to record a number of veterans for an embryonic oral archive also led to the purchase of a minidisk player worthy of a BBC interviewer.

Closer involvement with the TA and the Regular forces also led to the adoption of Army-style working dress, khaki trousers, boots and camouflage jackets. And the introduction of formal training with outside units meant a greater emphasis on rank, in public at least.

One of the chief characteristics of the late 20th and early 21st centuries has been the rise of the information society. This has been a mixed blessing for the Corps: it is of course immensely welcome since it has helped to publicize its continued existence, its ongoing achievements, its illustrious history and, not least, its search for new recruits. But it is also something of a curse, because the fast-moving and ephemeral nature of journalism makes for slick generalizations, a regrettable focus on glamour and, at worst, rank inaccuracies. Yet over the past two decades, the FANY have had regular (and gratifying!) outings in the media, appearing on *Woman's Hour* on Radio 4 and featuring in almost every more or less reputable publication imaginable.

In 1998, after seeing the Corps safely through seven years of change and consolidation, Anna Whitehead handed the torch to another 'outsider', Lynda Rose. Married to an Army officer, himself a fluent linguist, Mrs Rose's background in charity management was an appropriate preparatory school for leading an organization with high ambitions and restricted funds! Deputy Corps Commander Jenny Kauntze was the essential link at this time, providing the necessary continuity at HQ. Early the following year, her many years of exemplary service to the Corps were recognized by a certificate of commendation from the Commander-in-Chief UK Land Forces. Decia Stephenson meanwhile ran the records office, keeping track of members young and old, notifying HQ of any cases of hardship, and, during VE year, successfully completing the mammoth task of contacting all veteran FANYs to provide an account of their war work for the archives.

When Lynda Rose took over as Corps Commander in January 1998 her first letter to her unit summarized the concerns that now faced the FANY: 'Having had a very proper focus on our 90th Anniversary last year,' she began, 'we must now look again to the future, secure our financial position, and ensure that we relate our skills and talents to the requirements of the roles we have now, and those which will develop. Plans are in progress for us to expand our Casualty Bureau role; new opportunities with 2(NC) Signals Brigade are being examined; new language training schemes are in hand; our Constitution is being updated and our Rules and Regulations overhauled.' And finally, at a time of great unpredictability for all the forces, regular, reserve and voluntary alike, she continued: 'The recent Strategic Defence Review has settled much for the regular forces but created new uncertainties for the Reserves . . . cuts in manpower and in TAVRA accommodation will almost certainly affect us in future.'

What this meant, of course, was another impending move. After much soul-searching, a new home in the Right Wing of the Duke of York's Headquarters was found for the now traditionally itinerant Corps when it was forced to relocate in 2000 prior to the sale and demolition of Mercury House. The much-prized carpet was duly removed and cut to size to fit the smaller Mess!

In recent years, surviving FANY veterans have been interviewed for a number of high profile television documentaries about the work of SOE, both as agents in France and as the 'backroom girls'. In 1988 the television series *Wish Me Luck* dramatized the role of SOE women agents in France. Claire Rayner made her East End heroine Poppy a World War I FANY serving with a convoy in Flanders. Margaret Pawley, a former SOE FANY, interviewed many of her peers, and in her book *In Obedience to Instructions* has produced an accurate and enjoyable record of FANY service in North Africa, the Middle East and Italy. Canadian television recently screened a documentary about Joan Bamford Fletcher, a FANY serving with South East Asia

Command who took on the Japanese Army and Indonesian rebels to rescue a large number of prisoners of war. And in 2002, media interest about the FANY wartime contribution reached fever pitch during the release of the feature film *Charlotte Gray*, which is about a fictional FANY who is parachuted into occupied France. Throughout, the Corps has tried to maintain control of the flow of information reaching the media; one way it has done so is through its own excellent website (www.fany.org.uk) and an SOE sister site (www.64-baker-street.org) with which it is linked.

Meanwhile, in 1999, more changes took place. The Corps had been known as the Women's Transport Service (FANY) since 1937. In addition to the ribaldry to which the acronym gives rise these days (and which every FANY learns to accept with a wan smile), there is the fact that it no longer accurately describes what the Corps does. Members are certainly not 'nurses', nor are they even primarily 'First Aiders', although they are of course required to hold current First Aid certificates, and they are definitely not 'Yeomanry'. Nor are the skills of the Corps any longer concentrated merely in transport. So after much discussion and a ballot of members, it was decided with the agreement of their Commandant-in-Chief to change the name to FANY (Princess Royal's Volunteer Corps). However, the letters PRVC do not trip lightly off the tongue, and so the name FANY has stuck. Along with the new designation came yet another modification to the working dress: a smart beret with an attractive cap badge (designed in-house!) which will further help to align FANY members in the field with other units.

In early 2000 there came the following announcement: 'As you may know, a FANY medal was struck after the Great War: since then there has not been an award to recognize service to the Corps . . . . Thanks to the generosity of Captain David Whitehead, Royal Navy, and Mrs Anna Whitehead and another anonymous donor, we will be in a position soon to award a medal for ten years' or more meritorious service in peacetime. In line with the Territorial Army, our volunteers give very generously of their time to provide a trained resource for emergencies, but because of our independent status we do not qualify for territorial decorations.' The Princess Royal was presented with the first of these medals.

By early 2003 the Corps will have said a final farewell to the Duke of York's and moved, carpet, regimental silver and all, to even smaller – though immensely congenial and perhaps more permanent – accommodation at the Headquarters of the London Scottish Regiment in Horseferry Road.

Continuity through change? As the Corps sails towards its centenary in 2007, it is quite likely that despite all the changes that have taken place since those far-off days in 1907, its founding members would still recognize the First Aid Nursing Yeomanry in its current form. Much of the original groundwork, together with the refinements that Lilian Franklin introduced in the 1920s, has proved valid. Captain Baker's Constitution for his First Aid Nursing Yeomanry was flexible enough to give the Corps considerable freedom of action; the Regimental Board, a committee of serving officers, still governs the day-to-day running of the Corps; and the influential military and civilian members of the Advisory Council, under the Chairmanship of Major-General Patrick MacLellan, remains the final arbiter on policy. It is even still under royal patronage, for, within six months of the death of Princess Alice, The Princess Royal had agreed to become Commandant-in-Chief.

The office is run, as it always has been, by a minuscule and hard-working staff consisting of the Commanding Officer, the Deputy Corps Commander, the Adjutant, a Records Officer and a handful of part-time volunteers. In addition to the administration of the Active Corps and its emergency responsibilities, headquarters is the focus of the wider membership of over 600 subscribers. All other posts – Quartermaster, Training Officer, Finance Officer and so on – are filled mainly by the more senior of the active members, also, of course, working in their spare time. Although a certain number of FANY members become less active by reason of such natural accidents of life as getting married, having children or moving away from London, few do so for less cogent reasons, and practically no one actually resigns. Moreover, the annual advertisements in the national press and by word of mouth bring in a regular quota of applicants.

In spite of nearly 60 years without a major war, in spite of all the pressures that have compelled contraction and a changing role, the Corps' quintessence remains recognizably the same as it has always been: sturdy, versatile, idiosyncratic – and unique. If one thing above all shines through the 96 years of the Corps' history, it is the pride which its members feel in it. The FANYs have always felt, occasionally to the irritation of those less fortunate, that they were members of an elite, and this sense of belonging to something rather special endures. Like a good ship or a good regiment, the Corps has the enviable knack – perhaps inherited from its original association with the Guards – of inspiring in its members an intense loyalty to itself and all it stands for. For as long as that lasts, the FANY (PRVC) will continue to contribute its own slim, vivid strand to the weave of our national life.

Appendix I

List of major events since 1983

1983: New role in Army Communication Centres (Commcens).
1984: Co-option onto TAVRA for Greater London. **1985:**
Commandant in Chief dines with Corps and receives bound copy
of "F.A.N.Y." by Hugh Popham. **1986:** Participation in Lord
Mayor's Show on theme "Our Role in the City". **1987:** Emergency
team at Bishopsgate Casualty Bureau following hurricane. **1988:**
Royal Signals Permanent Staff Administrative Officer (PSAO) allo-
cated to HQ to assist with Commcen administration. Linguists at
London Congress of International Confederation of Reserve
Officers (CIOR). **1989:** "Marchioness" disaster: emergency team
deployed. Linguists at Centenary Conference of the Inter-
Parliamentary Union.

1990: Anna Whitehead takes over as Corps Commander on retirement of Sheila Parkinson. Odette Hallowes at commemoration of
50th Anniversary of institution of The George Cross. **1991:** Cannon
Street train crash: emergency team called out. Gulf War: operators
deploy to Army Casualty Cell, Empress State Building, London,
and to Chatham Commcen: teams on 24-hour watch for duration:
two FANYs serve in Gulf with Red Cross. Corps Commander lays
wreath at inauguration of SOE Memorial, Valencay. **1992:** Bomb at
St. Mary Axe: operators on duty over 4 days answering 3600 telephone calls. **1993:** Bishopsgate bomb: emergency team deployed.
The Princess Royal opens new Corps HQ at Mercury House, Duke
of York's Headquarters. Memorial plaque unveiled at Ravensbruck
to commemorate SOE (including FANY) agents who died there. **1994:**
Year of the Yeomanry (200th anniversary): The Queen takes salute
at review in Windsor Great Park. The FANY in mounted contingent
and parading on foot. 50th Anniversary of D-Day: representatives
in SHAEF Commemoration Parade, Bushy Park and at D-Day
Garden Party, Southwick House, Portsmouth. **1995:** 50th anniversary of VE/VJ Days: Corps members at all National ceremonies and
services. The Duke of York opens refurbished Duke of York's

Headquarters: visits FANY contingent. Death of Odette Hallowes, GC, a Vice President of the Corps. **1996:** The Princess Royal attends Open Day: unveils portrait of Maud MacLellan, Corps Commander 1947-1964, and accepts the "Odette"gift of silver on behalf of the Corps. FANY team flies to Benbecula, Western Isles, on exercise with a unit of The Parachute Regiment. The FANY in British Units contingent, Festival Parade, Leiden Holland. **1997:** Corps Commander Anna Whitehead awarded OBE. FANY team crosses Central Pyranees via WWII escape route: others support 46 Signal Squadron on marathon exercise in Derbyshire. Four-day expedition to France and Flanders visits battlefields and location where FANYs were based in WWI. The Princess Royal attends 90th Anniversary Service of Commemoration at the Guards Chapel, and Cocktail Party at Royal Hospital Chelsea.

1998: Lynda Rose takes over as Corps Commander on retirement of Anna Whitehead. FANYs drive tanks at Bovington, walk the Via Tilman in the Italian Dolomites, and assist with CIOR. Poppies are laid at the grave of Eveline Shaw, WWI FANY who died of dysentry in 1918 at Sezanne, Champagne-Marne: dedication of plaque to Odette Hallowes GC at the FANY Memorial, St. Paul's Knightsbridge. **1999:** The Princess Royal agrees new title for the Corps "FANY(Princess Royal's Volunteer Corps)". Exercise in Denmark with a Royal Signals squadron. "South Pole 2000" (the all-women expedition) launched from Duke of York's Headquarters. Membership of City of London TAVRA confirmed. **2000:** Dedication of plaque to Eveline Shaw on the FANY memorial, London: unveiling of memorial to Violette Szabo at Sussac, Limousin, France. Farnborough Air Show: teams support 256 Field Hospital in emergency hospital facility. The Princess Royal attends Open Day and receives the first honorary FANY medal. SOE's 60th anniversary commemoration at Beaulieu: veterans and uniformed FANYs attend. Polish Unit veterans and uniformed FANYs at unveiling of statue to General Sikorski in London. Hatfield train derailment: emergency team called out. FANYs return to Denmark on exercise with a Royal Signals squadron. Hon. Colonel presents FANY Long-Service medals. 50th Birthday celebration for the Princess Royal at Windsor Castle: Hon. Colonel, CO, DCC and Quartermaster attend. Death of Sue Ryder (Lady Ryder of Warsaw). **2001:** Death of Major General Charles Page, a Vice

President and former Hon. Colonel and Chairman of the Advisory Council. Formal role with 2(National Communications) Signal Brigade confirmed. Memorial to Voilette Szabo unveiled in Stockwell. SOE FANYs return to Apulia, Southern Italy. September 11th atrocity in New York:emergency team called out to assist the Metropolitan Police in support of the Foreign Office. Four FANYs on Household Cavalry mounts take part in Lord Mayor's Show. **2002:** The Princess Royal opens the London end of the Army Casualty Cell at FANY Headquarters. Commander Frances Blois elected Lord Mayor of Westminster. Potters Bar train crash:emergency team called out. Death of Sheila Parkinson, Corps Commander 1964-1990. Uniformed FANYs provide Guard of Honour for Prince of Wales at premiere of "Charlotte Gray". Deployment to Loir-Cher to commemorate the 60th anniversary of the first two FANY agents of SOE (de Baissac and Borrel) to parachute into France. Six FANYs parachute onto the DZ (drop zone) watched by Lise Villameur (de Baissac) who receives her French wings from Commandant of Parachute School at Pau: service and wreath-laying at memorial in Romorantin. Up-dating the Constitution of the Corps reaches its final stage. Teams deploy to London District Ops Room on 24-hour liaison with media-ops for duration of Firefighters' strike.

Appendix II

HONOURS AND AWARDS

1914–1918

Military Medal	19	Croix de Guerre	27
Legion of Honour	1	OBE	2
Ordre de la Couronne	1	MBE	2
Ordre de Leopold Chevalier	2	Mention in Despatches	11

1939–1945

George Cross	3	King's Commendation	1
George Medal	2	Chevalier de Légion d'Honneur	1
CBE	1	Croix de Guerre (WTS/FANY)	6
OBE (FANY/ATS)	6	(WTS/FANY EX WAAF)	6
(WTS/FANY)	6	Médaille de la Reconnaissance	2
MBE (FANY/ATS)	8	Norwegian Liberty Medal	1
(RAMC)	1	American Bronze Star	1
(WTS/EA)	2	US Medal of freedom	1
(WTS/FANY)	23	Mention in Despatches	36
(WTS/FANY ex WAAF)	2	BEM	10
King's Medal	1	Commendation for Good Service	2

Post-1945

OBE

M.L. MacLellan	Birthday Honours 1957
S.Y. Parkinson	Birthday Honours 1977
A. Whitehead	New Year Honours 1997

Appendix III

SENIOR OFFICERS OF THE CORPS

President, later Commandant in Chief
1933–81   Her Royal Highness The Princess Alice Countess of
Athlone, VA, GCVO, GBE

Commandant in Chief
1981–   Her Royal Highness The Princess Royal GCVO

Colonel in Chief, later Honorary Colonel
1922–33   General Sir Evan Carter, KCMG, CMG, MVO

Honorary Colonels
1933–46   Major General Sir Evan Gibb, KBE, CB, CMG, DSO
1946–50   Field Marshal The Rt Hon The Earl Wavell, PC, GCB,
GCSI, GCIE, CMG, MC
1952–58   Major General Sir Julian Gascoigne, KCVO, CB, DSO
1959–71   Major General Sir William Scott, KCMG, CB, CBE
(dual role as Chairman of Advisory Council 1965–70)
1971–76   Major General Sir John Anderson, KBE
1977–93   Major General Charles Page, CB, MBE, DL
1993–96   Major General Robert Cook MSc, M Phil
1996–   Major General Stephen Carr-Smith

Chairman of The Advisory Council and Colonel in Chief
(later Honorary Colonel)
1927–33   General Sir Evan Carter, KCMG, CMG, MVO

Chairmen of The Advisory Council
1933–34   Lieutenant General Sir Hugh Jeudwine, KCB, KBE
1935–65   The Rt. Hon. Lord Oaksey, PC, DSO, TD, DL (formerly
Sir Geoffrey Lawrence)
1965–72   Major General Sir William Scott, KCMG, CB, CBE
(dual role as Honorary Colonel 1965–70)
1972–87   Colonel Andrew Croft, DSO, OBE
1987–93   Major General Sir John Anderson, KBE
1993–97   Major General Charles Page, CB, MBE, DL
1998–   Major General Patrick MacLellan, CB, CVO, MBE

Appendix III

COMMANDING OFFICERS

1918–32   Lilian Franklin OBE
1932–30   Mary Baxter Ellis CBE (Seconded as Deputy Director ATS 1939–45)
1939–46   Marion Gamwell OBE (London HQ FANY Units)
1934–47   Marjorie Kingston-Walker (Deputy Corps Commander) (Seconded to ATS – Senior Commander Motor Companies 1939–45)
1939–46   Hope Gamwell (Scotland HQ Polish Units)
1931–47   Lady Sidney Farrar MBE (East African Units)
1946–47   Mary Baxter Ellis CBE
1947–64   Maud MacLellan OBE TD
1964–90   Sheila Parkinson OBE
1990–97   Anna Whitehead OBE
1998–   Lynda Rose

BIBLIOGRAPHY

Barnett, Correlli, *Britain and her Army* (Allen Lane 1970)

Beauchamp Washington (née Waddell), Pat, *FANY Went to War*

——, *Eagles in Exile*

Beevor, G., *SOE: Recollections and Reflections 1940–45* (Bodley Head 1981)

Bidwell, Shelford, *The Women's Royal Army Corps* (Leo Cooper 1977)

Binney, Marcus, *Women who Lived for Danger* (Hodder 2002)

Brittain, Vera, *Testament of Youth* (Fontana Paperbacks 1979)

Butler, Ewan, *Amateur Agent* (Harrap 1963)

Carew, Tim, *Wipers* (Hamish Hamilton 1974)

——, *Of Their Own Choice* (Hodder & Stoughton 1952)

Churchill, Peter, *Duel of Wits* (Hodder & Stoughton 1953)

Churchill, Winston Spencer, *The River War* (New English Library 1973)

Condell, Diane, & Liddiard, Jean, *Working for Victory* (Routledge 1987)

Dodds-Parker, Douglas, *Setting Europe Ablaze* (Springwood Books, 1983)

Ensor, R.C.K., *England 1870–1914* (Oxford 1949)

Escott, Beryl, *20th Century Women of Courage* (Sutton 1999)

Ewing, Elizabeth, *Women in Uniform* (Batsford 1975)

Farman, Christopher, *The General Strike* (Hart-Davis 1972)

Foot, M.R.D., *SOE in France* (HMSO 1965)

Forster, Mark Arnold, *The World at War* (Collins 1973)

Goldsmith, John, *Accidental Agent* (Leo Cooper 1971)

Hamond, Robert, *A Fearful Freedom* (Leo Cooper 1984)

Jones, Liane, *A Quiet Courage* (Bantam 1990)

King, Stella, *Jacqueline* (Arms and Armour 1989)

Kramer, Rita *Flames of the Field* (Michael Joseph 1995)

Lewin, Ronald, *Ultra Goes To War* (Hutchinson 1978)

Liddell Hart, B.H., *History of the First World War* (Cassell 1970)

Macdonald, Lyn, *The Roses of No Man's Land* (Michael Joseph 1980)

Marks, Leo, *Silk and Cyanide* (HarperCollins 1998)

Marshall, Bruce, *The White Rabbit* (Pan Books 1980)

Millar, George, *Maquis* (Mayflower 1973)

Minney, R.J., *Carve Her Name With Pride* (Collins Paperback 1964)

Nicholas, Elizabeth, *Death Be Not Proud* (Cresset Press 1958)

Oliver, Beryl, *British Red Cross in Action* (Faber 1966)

Ottaway, Susan, *Violette Szabo* (Leo Cooper 2002)

Pawley, Margaret, *In Obedience to Instructions* (Leo Cooper 1999)

Petrie, Sir Charles, *Scenes of Edwardian Life* (Eyre & Spottiswood 1965)

Robert, Cecil, *Life in Edwardian England* (Batsford 1969)

Saunders, Catharine, *Odette Churchill – In Her Own Time* (Hamish Hamilton 1989)

Sweet Escott, Bickham, *Baker Street Irregular* (Methuen 1965)

Taylor, A.J.P., *The First World War* (Hamish Hamilton 1963)

Walters, Anne-Marie, *Moondrop to Gascony* (Pan 1951)

Ward, Irene, *FANY Invicta* (Hutchinson 1955)

Unpublished sources

Archives of the Women's Transport Service (FANY)

Ashley Smith, Grace, *Diary 1909–19* (Imperial War Museum)

Hutchinson, Beryl B., *The Calais Convoy* (Imperial War Museum)

——, *The St Omer Convoy* (Imperial War Museum)

Privately printed

Tennent, R.J., *Red Herrings of 1918*

INDEX

Cluff, Reverend William, 32–3, 37, 48, 85
Cole-Hamilton, Margaret, 12, 24, 32–3, 35–6, 49, 134
Colston, Tony, 122, 136
Command Mixed MT Companies, 70
Commonwealth Parliamentary Association, 120
Convoys, 23–46, 117
Cook, Major General Robert see *Appendix III*
Cornioley, Henry, 104
Courage Trophy, 126, 129, 143
Crockett, Adele, 24–5, 49
Croft, Colonel Andrew see *Appendix III*
Cunningham, General, 80
Cyprus, 79

D-Day, 71, 104, 108, 123, 148
Dachau, 102, 127–8
Damerment, Madeleine, 99, 102, 128
Darcy, Kathleen Maclean, 6
de Baissac, Claude, 104
de Baissac, Lise (Villameur), 103, 150
Defence (Women's Forces) Regulations 1941, 63fn
Denmark, 139
Dictionary of National Biography (DNB), 149–150
Dieppe, 70
Dieu-Donné, Colonel, 38–9
Dismore, Lieutenant Colonel Leonard, 151
Ditte, General, 29
Dixon, Jean, 82
Dodds-Parker, Sir Douglas, 88, 93–4, 121

Driver Training Centre: *see* Camberley
Drummond, Joan, 128
Duke of York's Headquarters: *see* First Aid Nursing Yeomanry – Headquarters

Ebden, Doctor, 58
École des Troupes Aéroportées (ETAP), 150
Egypt, 79
Elizabeth, HM Queen (later Queen Elizabeth The Queen Mother), 115, 147
Elizabeth, HRH Princess (later HM The Queen), 68, 122, 144–5, 148–9
Emergency Service, 60–2
Epernay, 37, 42
Equestrian events, 143, 145
Ex HAMMER, 142
EX RUNNEL STONE – Denmark, 139
EX WINTEX, 138
Expeditionary Force Canteens, 32

FANtastics or Kippers, 30, 45
FANY/ATS, 61–4, 69–72, 79, 114, 116–17, 123
FANY/ATS SHAEF Mixed Company Car Company, 71, 123
FANY Hostel, St. John's Wood Park, 108
FANY in France 2002, 150
FANY Welfare Unit SEAC (*see* ALFSEA)
Farnborough Air Show, 140
Farrar, Lady Sidney, 54, 64, 71, 79–80 *and Appendix IV*
Farriers Company, 145
Fawley Court, nr. Henley, 91
Finnish Unit, 74, 134